PRAISE FOR

Witness to the Promised Land

"It's a fascinating look at a bygone era when political compromise, civility and moderation were the norm in Washington, rather than today's toxic atmosphere of partisan warfare, the nuclear option and legislative deadlock."

— **Albert Eisele,** *The Hill*

"John Stewart has written a book that reminds us what politics in America used to be, how much our democracy was able to do when men and women of commitment worked together for the common good, and how much we have lost in recent years. I enthusiastically commend it to people who are determined not to lose hope in these difficult times."

— **Walter F. Mondale**, Former Vice President of
the United States

"John Stewart, an architect of the historic Civil Rights Acts of the 1960s, has provided a vital public service by reminding us how those great popular victories for expanding freedom were won. And now—at a time of deep and bitter divisions in the nation's politics—Stewart offers clear-eyed and wise advice on how progressives once again can regain the initiative to unite the country in support of moral values in the best tradition of American democracy. Stewart has issued a clarion call for a return to politics based on civilized debate, moderation, and compromise."

— **Nick Kotz,** Pulitzer Prize Winning Journalist
Author, *Judgment Days*

"As a graduate student of the University of Minnesota and a Golden Gopher, I was a fan of Humphrey and John Stewart was his man! This book is a blueprint for preserving optimism in challenging times."

— **Patricia Schroeder**, Former Congresswoman from
Colorado; President & CEO of the Association of
American Publishers

"John Stewart brings us back to what we Americans could be as a people when we work to fulfill our rights and make civil rights real. As Americans who were engaged in the struggle, we used our power to speak up and act by working to make our country free and equal, inclusive and respectful. As a young lobbyist working on the 1964 Civil Rights Act, I can feel John Stewart making those heady days alive for me once more with his trenchant Christianity & Crisis articles and his contemporary insightful comments. As we get ready for the civil rights struggle, to extend the Voting Rights Act in 2007, a new generation of activists can learn from the earlier struggles by absorbing John Stewart's gift of *Witness to the Promised Land.*"

— **David Cohen,** Co-Chair, Advocacy Institute
President, Common Cause 1975–1981

"**Witness to the Promised Land** reaffirms that a politics based on community values transcends modern liberalism and conservatism. These essays reveal themselves to be startlingly relevant to our time and deserve our careful reading and attention."

> — **Mitchell J. Freedman**, Author, *A Disturbance of Fate*; Finalist, Sidewise Award for Best Alternative History, 2004

"John Stewart gives us a rarely seen insider's view of the dedication, legislative competence, and persuasive ability of a handful of Congressional leaders and their aides that finally gave birth to the momentous Civil Rights Act of 1964 and the Voter Rights Act of 1965. It is an exciting and moving story."

> — **Reverend William Sloane Coffin**, Chaplain, Yale University 1958–1975, Senior Minister, The Riverside Church 1977–1987

"I got to know John Stewart during the 'civil rights movement" (we called it the "Freedom Movement" then). Stewart demonstrated how insiders in government, like himself, and outsiders, who marched, demonstrated and sometimes got arrested, could work together effectively. I was definably an outsider, but Stewart was an insider, a key aide to Hubert Humphrey. This book allows but a riveting glance inside, and not just during the hectic years of the Freedom Movement. He shows how skill, patience, conviction and sometimes luck, were all needed to get worthwhile things done. Stewart was there and he writes engagingly. A great read!"

> — **Professor Harvey Cox,** Harvard Divinity School

" . . . I was terribly dependent then...on a young man on my staff, John Stewart. While he was not a senator, of course, his role was absolutely crucial, and without him I could not have done the things I needed to do to persuade, conciliate and advocate. Whenever I think of how dependent we are on others for our success, I am compelled to think of John during those difficult months. For endless hours thorough endless days, whenever I needed him, he was there with ideas, strategy, new language. He co-ordinated staff assistants of other pro-civil rights senators at daily strategy sessions and worked closely with outside civil rights lobbyists. While many people are important to the passage of major legislation and few are really so basic that the legislation would fail without them, the civil rights bill of 1964 would not have been the same without him. I know certainly that I would not have been able to work as well, and had I performed as floor leader significantly less well, the bill could have failed."

> — **Vice President Hubert H. Humphrey,** *The Education of a Public Man, My Life and Politics* (Doubleday, 1976)

Witness to the Promised Land

Observations on Congress and the Presidency
from the pages of *Christianity & Crisis*

To Bill Willis —
One g the great seekers
g the Promised Land here
in Tennessee —
John Stewart

John G. Stewart
with Foreword by Wayne H. Cowan

SⱠP

SEVEN LOCKS PRESS

Santa Ana, California

Seven Locks Press
P.O. Box 25689
Santa Ana, CA 92799
(800) 354-5348

Individual Sales. This book is available through most bookstores or can be ordered directly from Seven Locks Press at the address above.

Quantity Sales. Special discounts are available on quantity purchases by corporations, associations, and others. For details, contact the "Special Sales Department" at the publisher's address above.

Printed in the United States of America

Library of Congress Cataloging-in-Publication Data
is available from the publisher
ISBN 1-931643-64-4

Cover and interior design by Heather Buchman

To Hubert H. Humphrey
and many colleagues through the years
who shared his joyful optimism
"without apology, about this country and
about the American experiment in democracy."

— *(quotation is taken from Hubert H.*
Humphrey's grave marker in Minneapolis)

TABLE OF CONTENTS

FOREWORD

The year 1940 was devastating as the Nazis overran Europe, first the Netherlands, then Belgium, and finally France. The democratic civilization of the North Atlantic nations was on the block. Yet in the United States the isolationists and the pacifists, still mired in the memory of World War I, insisted that the new conflict was none of our affair. Out of nowhere early in 1941, *Christianity and Crisis (C&C)*, a simple, eight-page biweekly journal appeared.

These words appeared in its first editorial: "The tragic irony of this hour is that so many of the men in America whom this revolt against Christian civilization most concerns seem to be least aware of its implications. The freedom of these men to speak and write depends upon the existence of a certain type of civilization. Yet they talk and act as if they believed that, whoever wins, religion-as-usual, like business-as-usual, will be the order of the day. . . . The choice before us is clear. Those who choose to exist like parasites on the liberties that others fight to secure for them will end by betraying the Christian ethic and the civilization that has developed out of that ethic."

The prime founder of *C&C* was Reinhold Niebuhr, whom Hans Morganthau once described as "the greatest living political philosopher of America, perhaps the only creative political philosopher since Calhoun." Niebuhr moved readily from the theological to the political realm and was widely admired and followed in intellectual circles. From the beginning, it was his intention to seek out the implications of Christian faith for dealing with the problems of life in modern society, and *C&C* was his prime journalistic focus for doing so. Niebuhr attracted articles from outstanding persons in many fields, including

Alan Paton, Martin Niemoller, Tom Wicker, Lewis Mumford, Adlai Stevenson, Karl Barth, Herbert Butterfield, Denis de Rougemont, Harvey Cox, and George Kennan.

When the war ended, the nation's role in the world was largely consumed by the Cold War. On the domestic front, however, no problem was more urgent than that of race, an issue that had always deeply concerned the journal. From *C&C's* early years, Benjamin Mays, the president of Morehouse College, had been an important force on the journal's board. Following the 1954 Supreme Court decision on *Brown vs. the Board of Education*, *C&C* published a discerning, probing article by Frank P. Graham, a former U.S. Senator and president of the University of North Carolina. From then on the fat was in the fire and articles and editorials on the subject appeared regularly, often written by editors and others who were frontline veterans of freedom rides, jail sentences, and other forms of resistance to the nation's unjust racial system.

It was not until 1963, however, that *C&C* readers were treated to significant discernment of the Congressional legislative process that was so critical to ending legal segregation. John Stewart brought insights to the magazine based on his unique position as the prime legislative assistant to Hubert Humphrey; at the time, the Senate Whip was working vigorously for a bipartisan coalition to defeat the long intractable reign of the Southern "Dixiecrats." Humphrey was a hero to *C&C* editors and to most liberal thinkers and activists because of his humanist leadership in many areas of the nation's life. In addition, Humphrey and Niebuhr had long been close friends and allies in a number of endeavors, including the founding of Americans for Democratic Action.

John's position at Humphrey's side put him in the midst of the battle. With his keen eye and precise prose, John entered into the journal's pages a privileged inside view of how civil rights legislation was being crafted and advanced or thwarted by different factions. He gave readers close-up views of the major actors and detractors and described in detail the complex procedures and personalities of the Senate.

As he makes clear in pages of this book, racial inequality was the most significant domestic issue facing the country after World War II. And it concerned the religious community deeply. On no other issue has the Church spoken and acted more effectively. Up to that point in time the maxim for many church leaders was that politics and religion don't mix. Here was clearly a crossover point; never before had the mainline churches become so engaged in such significant lobbying and social action at so many levels. Leaders of the faith communities testified before Congressional committees, ecumenical state and local councils of churches provided information to grass roots supporters who deluged Congressmen and Senators with a massive outpouring of letters, and large delegations descended upon legislators' offices in the Capitol and in the streets of Washington and city and state capitols across the nation.

The churches, the African American community, organized labor, and the politicians who created the successful Congressional strategies joined forces. And as Clarence Mitchell, the able NAACP strategist, said at the time, they were all essential to the effort. Without the efforts of the religious community and the strong participation of the labor unions, he said, "I don't think we could have won . . . we needed everybody we had."

Only rarely do we have the benefit of the reporting and wisdom of someone like John Stewart who was on the scene and writing knowledgeably, firsthand. He wrote during three presidential administrations—Kennedy, Johnson, and Nixon—and was virtually looking over the shoulder of key figures—LBJ, Republican Minority Leader Everett Dirksen, and, of course, Hubert Humphrey—at especially nail-biting times during one of the nation's most climactic legislative struggles. He saw and vividly described Johnson's persuasive "magic," his capacity for legislative and Presidential leadership, the bipartisan role of Dirksen, and the steady hand of Humphrey as he shepherded the Civil Rights Act of 1964 through to victory.

In addition, John wrote cogently about LBJ as President and his approach to the nation's problems, apart from the Vietnam War. He also brought to our pages his unique insights into the challenges facing Richard Nixon following his election as President in 1968.

John was also writing scholastically on these subjects for his Ph.D. dissertation, and those essays comprise the bulk of the chapters in the 1997 book, *The Civil Rights Act of 1964: The Passage of the Law That Ended Racial Segregation*, edited by Robert D. Loevy. This fact alone makes it particularly appropriate that this book of his writings is being published now, bringing a wider readership to his perceptive reporting.

I know of no greater pleasure in my years at *C&C* than my discovering John and encouraging him to offer his insights and experience in analyzing the important events of a half-dozen years in the middle of the 1960s and sharing his insights and gifts with our readership. *C&C* and its readers owed a large debt of gratitude to John Stewart for his cogent analysis and writing at a very crucial time in the nation's history. I am delighted that John has followed the urging of many to draw these materials together in a book, especially in these present perilous times, so that lessons learned in earlier struggles can become guides for sane choices today.

Wayne H. Cowan
South Hadley, 2004

ACKNOWLEDGMENTS

Where does one begin? I suppose with Chris Dowell and Spence Parsons who, as I have explained in the Introduction, caused me to examine seriously the challenging theology of Christian realism, as exemplified by the thought and writings of Reinhold Niebuhr. These insights are more relevant than ever in this era of triumphalist Republican doctrine that seems likely to launch this nation on a sea of troubles that will require a generation to repair. I thank Bruce Hanson, our assistant minister at the First Congregational Church in Washington, DC, for suggesting my name to Wayne Cowan, then editor of *Christianity & Crisis* and now a good friend of forty years. I appreciate Wayne's generous words in his Foreword more than I can say. Norman Sherman, a close friend from the Humphrey years, encouraged me to push ahead with this project and suggested Seven Locks Press, where he once reigned as editor, as a place to seek publication. Jim Riordan, now publisher of Seven Locks Press, has been a welcome source of encouragement, editorial insight, and marketing acumen that would warm the heart of any author.

I also thank Mary McNamara of Union Theological Seminary and Bill McKeown, attorney for the *C&C* estate, for their gracious permission to reprint my thirteen articles and the twenty-fifth anniversary speech by Vice President Hubert Humphrey.

As I make clear in the dedication of this volume, Hubert Humphrey is a central figure in this book and in my life. Were he only with us today. My many colleagues from the Humphrey years know who they are and know that I appreciate their wisdom, dedication, and affection more than I can ever say.

Finally, to my wife, Nancy, and my children, Michael and Cara, I thank you for joining with me in these years of challenge, accomplishment, and disappointment. You have been the rock on which all else has rested. You are truly The Promised Land of my life.

INTRODUCTION

On May 17, 2000, it was totally unexpected: the announcement on National Public Radio that two men in their early to late sixties had been arrested for the 1963 bombing of the Sixteenth Street Baptist Church in Birmingham, Alabama, that had killed four young girls: Cynthia Wesley, Addie Mae Collins, Carole Robertson, and Denise McNair. This was one of the pivotal events in 1963—along with the murder of Mississippi NAACP director, Medgar Evers, the kidnapping and murder of three civil rights workers during "Freedom Summer," and the March on Washington for Justice and Freedom—that finally had propelled the Kennedy Administration and the U.S. Congress into a serious assault on the edifice of legalized segregation. Now, thirty-seven years later, here was an attempt to bring the perpetrators of this horrendous crime to justice.

"I can't believe it," I said to my wife, Nancy. "I just can't believe it. After thirty-seven years . . . extraordinary." Since that unexpected announcement, a jury convicted Thomas Blanton, Jr., of murder and sentenced him to life in prison in May 2001. One year later, the same sentence was handed down for Bobby Frank Cherry. Justice, at long last, had been served.

It is hard to recapture the horror that gripped most people when the bombing took place. The other violent civil rights assaults of those years were directed against those pushing for racial justice. Shocking as these crimes were, they were committed against front-line fighters, adults who made a conscious decision to attack the barriers of discrimination and segregation. The Birmingham bombing, by contrast, was a totally random killing of four young girls attending church in their frilly taffeta dresses. Their only crime, in the eyes of the unknown bombers, was their race and their parents' decision to affiliate with the Sixteenth Street Baptist Church.

In the bombing's aftermath, it was no longer acceptable to temporize eternally on civil rights, to put things aside, to pretend that the status quo was somehow satisfactory. Although nearly a year would elapse before the Civil Rights Act of 1964 became law, it was the murder of the four Birmingham girls that made failure in the legislative struggle impossible to contemplate.

These unexpected recollections surrounding the church bombing, triggered by the arrest and indictment of the alleged bombers, also brought back memories of what I was doing in those tumultuous years. Starting in October of 1962, I worked in Senator Hubert Humphrey's office as his principal legislative assistant for domestic matters. (Previously, in 1961, I had spent five months in his office as an unpaid congressional fellow getting to know the senatorial ropes.) Since his election to the Senate in 1948, Humphrey had been leader of a handful of liberal Democrats and Republicans pushing for legislative action on civil rights. They had developed an extensive agenda of legislation—dealing with poll taxes, lynching, the Civil Rights Commission, job discrimination, voting rights, education, public accommodations, and the like—which usually fell by the wayside, even though Senator Lyndon Johnson had engineered passage of watered-down bills in 1957 and 1960. Now, with civil rights issues dominating the national agenda as never before, Humphrey's years of wandering in the Senate's civil rights wilderness seemed about to end. The Promised Land was in sight.

His fellow Democratic senators had also elected Humphrey as the assistant majority leader or whip. In this role, he backed up the majority leader, Mike Mansfield of Montana, and took charge of rounding up votes on key legislative issues. For these reasons, Humphrey's office became an informal command post for those seeking action on civil rights bills—both fellow senators and their staffs and external advocates, such as the Leadership Conference on Civil Rights. Due entirely to fortuitous circumstance, I found myself squarely in the middle of perhaps the most significant domestic issue since World War II to land on the Senate's doorstep.

It was only three years since I had finished my course work and qualifying exams for a Ph.D. degree in political science at the University of Chicago. The dissertation—dealing with the Senate majority leader—had yet to be written. Nancy and I had lived in Hyde Park, the Chicago neighborhood where the University is located, between the fall of 1957 and early summer of 1960 when we packed up our second-hand trailer, hitched it to our 1950 Ford, and headed to Washington, D.C., to begin my congressional fellowship.

During our years in Hyde Park, we became attracted to the Hyde Park Baptist Church where our best friend, Chris Dowell, was serving as assistant minister while he attended Chicago Divinity School and where an attractive and articulate man, E. Spencer Parsons, served as the senior minister. Due to our friendship with Chris and the compelling forthrightness of Spence Parsons, we found ourselves being drawn into the active life of the church, much to our surprise. We certainly had not come to the University of Chicago to become Baptists (Nancy and I having been brought up as Methodist and Congregationalist, respectively). But, little by little, that is exactly what happened. Things even progressed to the point where, upon Spence Parson's urging, we assented to being baptized by full immersion in a large water tank before the full congregation. Spence had been thinking that is was time for somebody in the congregation to take the Biblical plunge, so to speak. Clad totally in white, we helped Spence achieve his sacramental objective. Among other things, the baptism signaled our commitment to play an active role in the life of the Hyde Park congregation.

xviii   John G. Stewart

Not unlike most Ph.D. graduate students, I found myself sinking ever deeper into the life of academe in the sense that one had an obligation to explore the philosophical roots of knowledge, to probe for first causes, and to achieve intellectually rigorous positions on matters of significance. This natural tendency was heightened by the presence on the political science faculty of Professor Leo Strauss, the eminent political philosopher, who was waging all-out war on the new political science that measured, counted, and extrapolated. Strauss would have none of this. He grappled with more fundamental questions that go to the nature of political things: virtue . . . the good life . . . liberty . . . knowledge of the truth. His influence over the department was gigantic and even though I never became a true Strauss disciple (passing up the associated obligation to become fluent in Greek), I found myself looking to understand more clearly the philosophical underpinnings of current political issues.

These two realities—our growing involvement in the life of the Hyde Park Baptist Church and the search for underlying realities of American politics—came together suddenly in a new interest I developed in the relationships—linkages—between politics and religion. In addition, the frustrations and embarrassments associated with the final years of the Eisenhower presidency—stalemate in Congress, the U-2 incident, the launching of Sputnik, and related early U.S. failures in space—had caused me to shift my familial allegiance from the Republican Party to the Democrats, another element of the political questioning going around in my head. Spence Parson encouraged me to pursue these interests, suggesting various authors I should read: Reinhold Niebuhr, John Bennett, Harvey Cox, William Lee Miller, John A.T. Robinson, Dietrich Bonhoffer, James Pike, and many others. Eventually this reading and thinking produced a lay seminar on "Religion and Politics" that I offered for about a dozen intrepid souls at Hyde Park Baptist Church in the fall of 1959. The seminar went well. My interest in the ties between liberal Protestant Christianity and contemporary political matters continued to grow.

In the course of preparing materials for my seminar, I frequently ran across articles or opinion pieces in *Christianity & Crisis: A Christian Journal of Opinion*, a small but highly regarded biweekly publication founded by Reinhold Niebuhr in 1941. *C&C* as it was universally known, became an important source of non-pacifist, interventionist Christian thought as the shroud of Nazism descended across Europe. Christians had a moral obligation to oppose evil on the scale perpetrated by Hitler. Simply turning the other cheek was not an acceptable Christian response when the lives of millions of people, not to mention Western democracy itself, were at stake. *C&C* continued its interest in current political matters after the war. Its pages could always be counted on to deliver challenging, informed, and relevant points of view, not likely to be found elsewhere. These pages provided various readings for my Hyde Park seminar.

Thus I was truly delighted, indeed surprised, when *C&C*'s editor, Wayne Cowan, telephoned me one day in the early spring of 1963 to see if I might consider writing a short commentary for an upcoming issue of *C&C* on the current state of the battle for civil rights in Congress. Wayne had gotten my name from Bruce Hanson, assistant minister at Washington's First Congregational Church, and was checking things out. I wondered to myself what I might have to say that would be up to *C&C*'s standards. But I responded that I'd be pleased to try. This began a relationship that stretched from June 21, 1963, to January 20, 1969. During that period, I wrote thirteen pieces, covering such topics as civil rights, the nuclear test ban treaty, a critique of Senator Goldwater, the Great Society, Lyndon Johnson's presidency, the urban crisis, and, in the end, the incoming administration of Richard Nixon.

In every case, I was writing about issues in which I was personally engaged, hence cutting down on anything approaching serious "research." Without planning to do so, I managed to cover most of the key issues that dominated American politics in the 1960s, with the major exception of the Vietnam War. For much of this time, I was working in the office of then Vice President Humphrey. His contorted feelings over the war affected us all. I never felt I had anything especially noteworthy to contribute on this tragic issue and so I didn't. Two points are worth noting: The obvious awkwardness of commenting on current political and legislative matters, such as Vietnam, while working on the Vice President's staff caused me to invent a pseudonym, "Nicholas D. Picque," for five articles that appeared from 1965 to 1968. I figured the initials NDP could also signify "Nom de Plume," an artifice that only I appreciated.

Second, Humphrey's dogged public loyalty to Johnson's escalating war policy strained and, in some cases, ruptured his relations with many of his former allies and supporters who also were *C&C* subscribers or contributors. These strains came to the surface in an appearance he made in May 1966 at the twenty-fifth anniversary celebration of *C&C* held at the Riverside Church in New York City. Reinhold Niebuhr was to be especially honored, even though his failing health prevented him from attending in person. (Humphrey stopped by Niebuhr's apartment for a short visit on his way to Riverside Church.) Humphrey delivered a speech—with the usual number of spontaneous additions—that had been principally crafted by William Lee Miller, with a little help from me. He delivered it effectively but many in the audience sat on their hands when he talked about Vietnam. One can argue that this reticence among Humphrey's natural allies on an issue that Humphrey never could deal with effectively cost him the presidency two years later. Excerpts of Humphrey's speech are included in this volume.

Forty years later I've found it interesting to look back on these *C&C* contributions. They capture a perspective of many of the decade's major concerns that I witnessed, as played out on the grand stage of the nation's Executive and Legislative branches. These pieces express a lively optimism about the future of American democracy that today in the aftermath of the intervening years—not to mention the events of September 11, 2001—almost seems naïve. The disappointment and concern that today dominates the worldview of many persons who share my political and religious persuasion are wonderfully absent. Nonetheless, I concluded it would be worthwhile to bring these *C&C* articles together in one small volume, along with a few editorial comments, drawing on events and personal experiences that could not have been known when the articles were written. *C&C*'s long-time editor, Wayne H. Cowan, has graciously provided a foreword to this endeavor.

John G. Stewart
Knoxville, 2004

CIVIL RIGHTS LEGISLATION: REALITY REPLACES ROUTINE

In my initial piece for *Christianity & Crisis*—June 1963—I commented on the action that was beginning to build in Congress for meaningful action on civil rights. The liberal, pro-civil rights forces on Capitol Hill had become increasingly frustrated and irritated with President Kennedy and his administration. Recent legislative attempts had gone badly. The 1960 bill—submitted by President Eisenhower in 1959—focused on strengthening the voting rights provisions of the 1957 bill that Senate Majority Leader Lyndon Johnson had skillfully maneuvered through the Senate. This time, however, Johnson's legislative magic deserted him. The Southern Democrats scored a clear victory by emasculating the legislation of all meaningful content through a successful filibuster.

Things only got worse in 1962. This time President Kennedy proposed legislation to nullify the use of literacy tests to keep African-Americans from voting in Southern states. The Southern Democrats filibustered again. After two unsuccessful efforts to stop the filibuster by invoking cloture (a parliamentary device requiring a two-thirds majority), Senator Majority Leader Mike Mansfield surrendered and the legislation was set aside.

In addition, at the opening of the 88th Congress in 1963, the pro-civil rights forces had once again failed to modify the Senate rule that spelled out the cloture procedure so that a simple majority or a three-fifths majority could shut off a filibuster. This battle over Senate Rule XXII had been waged periodically since 1949 with the reformers always losing. The Kennedy administration provided little encouragement or support in these losing battles. Liberals of both parties despaired, even as events outside of Congress—freedom rides, sit-ins, voter registration drives—acquired a new urgency and force.

As my column notes, the administration had sent new proposals to Congress but the likelihood of meaningful action seemed distant. Then the graphic pictures and reports from Birmingham of demonstrators, many of them children, being attacked by police dogs and fire hoses, the bombing of Martin Luther King, Jr.'s motel room and the home of King's brother dramatized the urgency of a forceful response from the President. That came on the evening of June 11, 1963, when President Kennedy addressed the nation on television and announced his decision to send a meaningful omnibus bill to Congress. The die had been cast. President Kennedy was fully in the battle. And even as he spoke to the nation, a sniper was preparing to assassinate Medgar Evars, the Mississippi field secretary of the NAACP, in the early hours of June 12.

Congress awoke to discover it was time to go to work.

CIVIL RIGHTS LEGISLATION:
Reality Replaces Routine
C&C – June 24, 1963

THE TURBULENT EVENTS in Birmingham and other Southern and Northern cities have transformed what promised to be an unusually routine session of Congress into one potentially charged with emotion, conflict and an opportunity for historic accomplishment. Prior to these racial outbreaks the most disturbing aspect of the Congressional scene had been the failure of Congress to include on its active agenda the truly significant domestic issues of the day.

For a number of reasons the 88th Congress has been determined either not to pursue such essential questions or to consider them from a limited perspective that has made meaningful confrontation, struggle and decision most unlikely. The President's proposals for tax reduction and reform are but one illustration.

The vast challenge of urban blight and decay and the closely related question of adequate housing have been avoided except as these questions relate to the mass transit bill that passed the Senate in April. Hospital insurance for the elderly apparently has been scheduled for the second session. The comprehensive education bill has faltered before a remarkable combination of misfortunes. With the exception of a little noticed six-month study of unemployment conducted by Senator Joseph Clark, Congress simply has ignored major domestic issues.

It is not that the legislators have been idle. Worthwhile proposals in the areas of mental health, youth employment, mass transit, agriculture and medical education have passed one or both houses. But no person truly concerned with the historic social and economic transformations sweeping the nation could say that these bills, however desirable in their own right, represent forthright attempts by Congress to address itself to the most crucial questions of the day.

Until Birmingham, the most urgent of all domestic problems—the Negroes' struggle to achieve full civil equality—seemed destined for similar treatment. Like many other parts of the Administration's program, the three initial civil rights proposals were eminently desirable, but they still did not reflect the critical dimensions of the problem. One bill provided the Attorney General with badly needed legal tools in the area of voting rights, e.g., the appointment of Federal referees, the presumption of literacy upon completion of a sixth-grade education and preferential treatment for voting suits in the Federal courts. A second bill extended the U.S. Civil Rights Commission for an additional four years (in contrast to the earlier two-year extensions) and authorized a broadening of responsibility beyond the mere collection and publication of information. A third authorized the Federal Government to provide technical assistance for school districts attempting to desegregate *if* local school officials requested such assistance.

While passage of even these bills could not be guaranteed, most observers predicted some positive results, particularly on the voting and Civil Rights Commission measures. Southern opponents, especially in the Senate, would invoke the ritual of full debate but without fervor or commitment. In other words, Congress would again be spared a direct encounter with reality and the consequent ferment and turmoil.

Who bears responsibility for this insulation? Too often the blame is laid at the President's feet. Of course he has the prerogative to raise whatever issues he desires and in whatever dimensions he chooses. But the institutional and individual weaknesses of elected leadership in both houses are factors that cannot be ignored. The offices of Speaker of the House and Senate Majority Leader are positions with little inherent authority; the personal skill and resoluteness possessed by the various incumbents generally have determined the extent of their actual leadership. Currently Speaker John W. McCormack and

Majority Leader Mike Mansfield hesitate to initiate any challenge of committee chairmen leading to more direct confrontation with fundamental questions by the entire Congress.

Congress seemingly lacks the internal resources to initiate meaningful legislation. In point of fact, this is only a partial truth. Many far-sighted proposals are introduced entirely on Congressional initiative, but when leadership is lacking, as at present, the only proposals that reach the level of active consideration are those that receive the additional political leverage of Presidential support.

Civil rights is a good example. For many sessions members of both parties have introduced a broad spectrum of far-reaching civil rights measures. There have been several versions of the "Title III" provision stricken from the Civil Rights Act of 1957, which would authorize the Attorney General to seek an injunction whenever a person is denied the equal protection of the law. Other bills would establish a Fair Employment Practices Commission, enforce school desegregation and provide equal accommodations through the Interstate Commerce Clause of the Constitution. Their sponsors can only patiently await— or actively promote—the degree of Presidential involvement that will transform a bill into a live issue.

Such Presidential commitment is now a reality. The rapidly accelerating drive for civil equality has, quite unexpectedly, created the elements of a truly historic Congressional struggle. Seldom has any President become publicly committed to a course of action cutting so deeply into the social fabric of the entire nation. Never has the question of civil rights been raised with so few viable areas of compromise available to the President and his Congressional leaders. Above all else the President must fashion a truly bipartisan coalition for this battle; lacking this, he will be unable to obtain the twenty-four Republican votes necessary to end the anticipated Senate filibuster and the Republican votes necessary to bring the measure through the House Rules Committee.

The outcome of this struggle will be a major factor in determining who will be running the House and Senate in the immediate future. A victory for the President would enhance immeasurably the influence of elected leaders in both houses and diminish accordingly the influence of certain committee chairmen, principally Senator Richard Russell and Representative Howard W. Smith. Moreover, the personal and collective decisions reached during the forthcoming contest will have a definite impact on the Republican resurgence in the South, the choice of a Republican Presidential candidate in 1964 and the outcome of the Presidential election itself.

The Congress is at last stirring as reality takes the place of routine.

STALL ON CIVIL RIGHTS

The note of upbeat optimism that characterized my initial offering to *C&C* had vanished by the time it came to write my second—a little more than a month later.

The momentum generated by President Kennedy's stirring address to the nation dissipated rapidly when his omnibus bill encountered the political and procedural complexities of Capitol Hill. In part, the administration's relative conservatism in dealing with civil rights (out of fear that alienated Southern Democrats would stall other elements of the President's legislative program) reappeared when Attorney General Robert Kennedy sought to dampen down the strengthening proposals that were taking shape in the House Judiciary Committee, led by Rep. Emanuel Celler of New York. Dozens of civil rights proponents demanded to be heard in public hearings that ran into August. These proponents saw the President's bill as the long-awaited vehicle to achieve the oft-postponed civil rights agenda that had been building for decades.

The Attorney General initially could not control these various strengthening proposals to the omnibus bill (H.R. 7152)—a ban on discrimination in private employment, the old "Title III" stricken from the 1957 bill by Lyndon Johnson, and an expansion of the voting rights provisions to cover both Federal and state elections. Fearing that such a strengthened bill could never survive the rigors of a Southern filibuster in the Senate, Attorney General Kennedy finally reached a compromise with the bipartisan civil rights forces in the House. But more time had slipped away. The House Judiciary Committee reported the revamped—but still strengthened—H.R.

7152 to the full House of Representatives on November 20—two days before Harvey Lee Oswald struck down President Kennedy in Dallas.

The March on Washington in August that seemed so threatening to legislative leaders in early summer turned out to be one of the historic moments in the nation's civil rights struggle, always to be remembered for Dr. King's magnificent "I Have a Dream" oration. In Washington, white and black churches worked in harmony preparing for the event. On August 28, Nancy and I participated in a breakfast of leaders, including Senator Humphrey and marchers from across the country at the First Congregational Church. Later we stood among the huge gathering of peaceful participants and watched hundreds cool their feet in the waters of the Reflecting Pool. Not a single arrest was made.

The ascension of former Senate Majority Leader Lyndon Johnson to the Presidency brought new hope to the civil rights forces. His mastery of the Senate would surely lead him to a way to defeat the Southern Democrats' filibuster. His words to a joint session of Congress on November 27 seemed to commit himself and his administration to eventual victory: "No memorial oration or eulogy could more eloquently honor President Kennedy's memory than the earliest possible passage of the civil rights bill . . . We have talked long enough . . . We have talked for 100 years or more . . ."

But eight more months of talking would be needed to secure this memorial to the slain President.

STALL ON CIVIL RIGHTS

C&C – August 5, 1963

A variety of dangerous and disheartening obstacles currently confronts President Kennedy and his Congressional leaders as they strive to transform the omnibus civil rights bill into meaningful law.

The Congress is again showing its unique capacity for preserving a business-as-usual demeanor despite the urgent crisis at hand. Though members of Congress initially predicted passage of the civil rights bill in the House of Representatives by the last week of July, final action by Labor Day would now be quite an achievement. Whereas the Senate was expected to spend the month of August in the grip of a Southern filibuster, the forecasts of final Senate action now include references to Thanksgiving dinner and Christmas trees.

This situation is especially discouraging since opponents of civil rights have had little to do with this slowdown. Rep. Howard Smith, chairman of the House Rules Committee, has not yet refused to convene his committee in order to block—at least temporarily—consideration of the civil rights bill on the House floor. Neither has Senator James Eastland, chairman of the Judiciary Committee, prevented that body from reporting the bill to the Senate, nor has Senator Richard Russell assumed command of the Southern filibuster. All these delaying tactics, among others, still remain to be overcome.

The current situation is simply a result of Congressional refusal to buckle down to hard, sustained work and its unwillingness to revamp outmoded legislative machinery and traditions to permit prompt action in times of domestic crisis. Who can recall when Congress last defined a national emergency in terms of human rights?

In addition to Congressional torpidity, other developments are causing concern. While most people have focused their attention on the dangers of a Senate filibuster, the importance of steering the civil rights bill successfully through the House of Representatives deserves far more attention than it has received. This task will require great skill and determination; moreover, the outcome in the House will be the principal factor in determining the ultimate character of the legislation that goes to the White House. The House bill, for instance, will probably embody the most forceful civil rights legislation obtainable from this Congress. The opportunities to strengthen the bill in the Senate will be few indeed.

The goal in the Senate is to reach a point where the members will have the opportunity to vote for final passage of the bill. This entails either breaking a Southern filibuster by force or obtaining a two-thirds majority to terminate the filibuster by cloture.

To reach this point a plan is being considered that calls for complete acceptance of the bill as passed by the House. This would mean tabling every Senate amendment regardless of its individual merit. By this procedure all Southern amendments could be defeated by simple majority vote and without debate. If that is not possible, maximum strength could be mobilized behind the drive to obtain a two-thirds majority necessary to impose cloture. This strategy would avoid another chain of parliamentary pitfalls by eliminating the conference between the Senate and House members to resolve differences in their respective bills.

This plan for permitting no Senate amendments depends principally on passing a bill in the House that is acceptable to both the President and the supporters of civil rights in the Senate. If the House bill is seriously deficient in any major respect, the unity among liberal and moderate Senators of both parties would be difficult to maintain. Such unity is essential if the Southern filibuster is to be surmounted.

Moreover, the growing strain among Republicans casts the outcome of the civil rights effort in grave doubt. Conservative supporters of Senator Goldwater see their opposition to critical sections of the legislation (e.g., Federal enforcement of the right of equal access to public accommodations) as possibly providing the vehicle to capture the Southern and Western states that loom so prominently in the Goldwater Presidential strategy. Liberal Republicans, however, express deep concern over the possibility that the party of Lincoln may be transformed into a white man's party by these conservative tactics.

The resolution of the internal Republican struggle will have the profoundest impact on the fortunes of the legislation because 40–50 Republican votes for civil rights will be needed in the House and 22–24 in the Senate.

Since Republican votes are so critically important, many civil rights supporters in Congress view with sincere apprehension the demonstration planned in Washington during the last week of August. Despite the determination of the leaders organizing the demonstration to preserve law and order and the decision to keep the marchers from Capitol Hill, unexpected violence could still erupt precisely at the time the House is nearing final action on civil rights.

Such outbreaks would certainly jeopardize the support of many moderate Republicans whose votes are essential to victory. The loss of these votes in the House would presage a similar result in the Senate. A well-established rule-of-thumb for use with undecided legislators is to keep strictly to the merits of a bill as they determine their final positions; that is, never provide them with an easy out. A race riot in Washington might do just that.

A lethargic Congress, the importance of forceful House action, the inner conflict over civil rights among Republicans, and the forthcoming demonstrations are factors that dampen the optimism of those persons working for effective civil rights legislation. But still visible is the lone element that may ultimately prevail: the fact that success would officially mark the beginning of the end of second-class citizenship in America and would guarantee for President Kennedy and the 88th Congress a notable place in the history of this nation.

THE TEST BAN TREATY:
The "Great Debate" That Never Was

While the House Judiciary Committee geared up for consideration of President Kennedy's omnibus civil rights bill, an equally compelling policy initiative was taking shape in Moscow. The President had dispatched Gov. Averell Harriman to head the joint U.S./British delegation seeking to negotiate with the Soviet Union a treaty banning atmospheric nuclear tests. That such a termination served the interests of both sides of the Cold War was revealed when agreement was reached in late July. The treaty was initialed in Moscow before a bipartisan delegation of senators, and Kennedy decided to seek immediate ratification by the Senate (even as the House was struggling with his civil rights proposals).

When the President formally sent the treaty to the Senate in early August, its ratification was far from assured. Important Republican senators—Minority Leader Everett Dirksen and Bourke Hickenlooper of Iowa—had refused to join the official delegation traveling to Moscow. Arizona Senator Barry Goldwater talked suspiciously of "secret deals" that had been struck with the Soviets. Former members of the Joint Chiefs of Staff publicly opposed it. The Armed Services Committee, chaired by Senator Richard Russell of Georgia, issued a report highlighting the treaty's "serious military disadvantages." It was rumored that Russell would try to condition his support for the treaty on Kennedy's backing down on his civil rights demands.

In what turned out to be a preview of the strategy that eventually won passage of civil rights in the Senate the following spring, backers of the Limited Nuclear Test Ban Treaty—with the administration's active encouragement and support—organized a "Citizens' Committee for a Nuclear Test Ban" that mobilized external support: churches, universities, business, organized labor, and civic organizations. The focus of this external pressure was Minority Leader Dirksen since the two-thirds vote required for ratification was not achievable without Dirksen's assent, just as it would take a two-thirds vote to break a Southern Democratic filibuster during the civil rights debate. After a month or so of uncertainty, Dirksen revealed his decision to support the treaty in suitably dramatic fashion (presaging exactly the same performance with civil rights). The Senate consented to the treaty's ratification on September 24, 1963 by the decisive margin of 80–19.

This period also was hectic for the Stewart family. Several weeks prior to ratification, I reluctantly had to remove myself from the day-to-day battle and my role as Senator Humphrey's emissary to those working for the treaty's acceptance. I had agreed to be a visiting lecturer in government at Cornell University to teach the undergraduate course on the U.S. Congress during the fall semester.

So Nancy and I packed up our belongings and headed north to Ithaca, New York in early September. It was there, on November 22, while walking across the Cornell campus on my way to lunch, that I learned of President Kennedy's assassination. We spent that sad weekend with graduate school friends in Syracuse and there witnessed Jack Ruby's killing of Lee Harvey Oswald, live, on network TV. After that horror, we decided to drive to Washington and arrived in time to stand along Pennsylvania Avenue as the President's funeral cortege passed by and the pack of world leaders walked along, General DeGaulle towering over the diminutive Emperor Haille Salasse.

As my commentary in C&C pointed out, the debate over the treaty failed to live up to its advance billing as the greatest Senate debate since the World War I treaty establishing the League of Nations. But while it may have lacked substance, the debate's outcome was far more satisfactory from the President's perspective. The victory held out hope that a path out of the nuclear jungle could be found.

Forty years later we are still struggling to stay on that path.

THE TEST BAN TREATY:
The "Great Debate" That Never Was
C&C – October 14, 1963

Almost before anyone realized what was happening, a test ban treaty had been initialed and signed in Moscow and presented to the Senate for its advice and consent. Thus the summer doldrums on Capitol Hill were enlivened by a truly significant issue that would, it was confidently predicted, produce a "great debate" on U.S. Cold War, arms control and national security policy.

The treaty came to the Senate precisely at a moment in history when many of the basic assumptions relating to these policies appeared to be wearing a trifle thin, i.e., the inevitable growth of Western unity, the fundamental identity of interest between Communist China and the Soviet Union, and the reliability of the balance of nuclear terror to preserve the peace. Since the Soviet decision to sign the treaty was probably related to their re-evaluation of certain of these assumptions, the time appeared most propitious for the Senate to do likewise. The treaty debate would provide the ideal forum.

What went wrong? Why did the Senate spend most of the debate merely recounting and flaunting the military capability of the U.S., comparing the professional credentials of various scientific witnesses and playing one general off against another? What happened to the "great debate"?

For one thing, it fell victim to the extreme reluctance of Senators to participate actively in a debate that would suggest new concepts in the area of arms control and would imply the possibility of new relationships between the USA and the USSR. If Senator Joseph McCarthy's legacy to America was relegating public discussion of these questions to the most banal level, such a legacy may be more enduring than most persons realize. While only a handful of Senators subscribe to the Radical Right's obsession with "total victory" and the "no win" policy, few others are willing to move beyond the accepted slogans and notions concerning the Cold War, nuclear weapons and national security.

For years a handful of Senators, including Humphrey, Clark, Morse, Church and, more recently, McGovern, have kept these matters alive in Congress. The signing of a limited test ban treaty appeared to provide an opportunity to engage additional Senators in public discussion. Although many spoke on the treaty, what they said demonstrated little appreciation of the complex factors involved in preserving U.S. security in a volatile and rapidly changing world.

In addition, a struggle for status and influence between the Foreign Relations Committee and the Armed Services Committee further kept the debate from becoming either illuminating or productive in a long-term sense. The intimate relationship between military and foreign policy, particularly in the area of arms control, resulted in both committees actively seeking to capture the role of principal Senate authority in these decisions.

A test ban treaty would appear to fall within the jurisdiction of the Foreign Relations Committee. However, the Preparedness Subcommittee of the Armed Services Committee for the past year has been holding an intensive series of secret hearings relating to the proposed comprehensive test ban. The strong presumption has been that these hearings developed little testimony to support such a treaty and much by which to oppose it.

When a limited treaty unexpectedly became a reality in July, an immediate contest developed between Foreign Relations and Armed Services to determine: (1) which committee would control formal consideration of the treaty; and (2) which committee would define the issues to be debated. Although Foreign Relations, with Senator J. William Fulbright as chairman, managed to preserve jurisdiction over the treaty itself, Armed Services, under the generalship of Senator Richard Russell, kept the debate focused almost exclusively on the narrow military and scientific considerations.

Fulbright initially moved to cut off separate committee action by Russell and his colleagues on Armed Services (Thurmond, Stennis, Jackson, Goldwater, et al.) by inviting them to participate in the Foreign Relations Committee hearings. But Fulbright made it quite clear they would not participate in the formal vote to report the treaty to the full Senate. Fulbright's invitation was accepted, but Stennis also launched separate and secret hearings before his Preparedness Subcommittee.

At one point, Russell considered asking the Senate for formal referral of the treaty to Armed Services. Although this request was not forthcoming, the Preparedness group did release an "interim report" that emphasized the allegedly grave military disadvantages of the treaty. Fulbright did little to hide his extreme displeasure at this "encroachment" on the prerogatives of his committee.

Therefore, due largely to most Senators' preference to avoid broader issues, the debate revolved around the allegations of military disadvantages in the interim report, even though the Joint Chiefs of Staff had endorsed the treaty. Under these conditions the proceedings on the Senate floor assumed the character of a litany: alleged military risks raised, alleged risks denied, over and over. By the second week the debate had become almost unbearable.

What happens to the problems of the Cold War, arms control and national security now that the question of a test ban is no longer the dominant issue? Senator Clark has scheduled hearings on the economic impact of disarmament, and Senator McGovern is exploring ways by which the defense budget might be reduced in noncritical areas. The handful of other Senators who will join in these inquiries still face the prospect of talking about an unpopular subject to many disinterested and even hostile colleagues.

THE TESTING OF LYNDON B. JOHNSON:
Civil Rights in the Senate

The extensive delays in the House of Representatives' consideration of the Omnibus Civil Rights bill (H.R. 7152), a jammed legislative calendar in both houses, and the tumult associated with President Kennedy's assassination and the accession of Lyndon Johnson to the presidency resulted in the legislation not passing the House until February 10, 1964. During this period, civil unrest and violence grew across America (the Birmingham church bombing killing the four young girls took place on September 15, 1963). The stakes associated with the bill's enactment grew larger and larger with each violent event.

Although passage in the House took about six months longer than initially anticipated, the result was worth waiting for. A robust coalition of Democrats and Republicans strengthened in many fundamental ways the legislation President Kennedy had dispatched to Capitol Hill the previous June. Today—almost forty years later—when conservative Republican domination of the House is almost taken for granted, it is interesting to note that fully 78 percent of House Republicans supported H.R. 7152 in its strengthened form, compared to 59 percent of the Democrats.

The nation's eyes were now fixed squarely on the new President. Having demonstrated his mastery of the Senate during his years as majority leader, Johnson, it was assumed, would surely figure out some way to get the House-passed bill through the Senate, essentially intact.

This assumption is examined in some detail in my article that appeared in the March 2, 1964 edition of *C&C*. The article drew on much of the research on Johnson that I had assembled as part of my Ph.D. dissertation on the Senate majority leadership that I was writing for the University of Chicago. The dissertation was not to be completed until 1967 and, by then, I had decided to use the Senate's consideration of the civil rights legislation as an extended portion of the manuscript. These chapters were to provide, verbatim, most of the text related to Senate passage in *The Civil Rights Act of 1964: The Passage of the Law that Ended Racial Segregation*, edited by Robert D. Loevy and published by the State University of New York Press (1997).

Nancy and I arrived back in Washington from our fall semester at Cornell just as the House was finally completing floor action on H.R. 7152. I immediately found myself thrust into preparations for the Senate's consideration. My boss, Senator Hubert H. Humphrey, as majority whip and long-time civil rights advocate, had been appointed floor manager of the legislation when it arrived from the House. My good fortune was that, as his assistant on domestic legislation, I found myself squarely at the center of all strategy sessions of the bipartisan civil rights forces and as principal liaison with all external groups working for passage.

My contributions to *C&C* on the bill's passage—comprising the next three pieces—were written from this privileged position on the inside—an exceptionally fortuitous turn of events for me and, I suppose, for *C&C*.

CIVIL RIGHTS IN THE SENATE
The Testing of Lyndon B. Johnson
C&C – March 2, 1964

HOUSE PASSAGE of the long-awaited civil rights bill has set the stage for the most climactic legislative struggle to occur on Capitol Hill in many years: consideration of this same bill by the United States Senate. Simultaneously, Lyndon B. Johnson is being confronted with the greatest personal test of political leadership in his almost three decades of wheeling and dealing in Washington.

During his highly publicized tenure as Senate majority leader (1955–1960), Johnson frequently would expound on how one gets things done on Capitol Hill. "The first thing a politician must learn," he would observe, "is how to divide any number by two and add one."

"What do you want," he would often admonish his more impatient liberal Democratic colleagues, "houses or a housing issue? Civil rights legislation or a civil rights issue?" And then there was the best-known Johnsonism of all: "Politics, my friends, is the art of the possible."

Considering the fractional nature of his Democratic majority, Johnson's accomplishments during a Republican administration testified to the wisdom contained in these folksy nostrums; the successful leader in Congress had to recognize the value of accommodation, negotiation, compromise and the *quid pro quo*. Johnson's ability to "trade apples for orchards" (as Senator Pat McNamara used to say) further enhanced the attractiveness of this approach.

Fewer Apples to Trade

Yet the drama of the impending encounter in the Senate stems directly from the fact that Johnson is no longer the majority leader and, as President, finds himself with far fewer "apples" to trade. The civil rights bill that passed the House is the most comprehensive and hard-hitting omnibus bill ever approved; yet there is not one section that can be classified as expendable. The elimination of the bill's two more prominent features—the public accommodations section (Title II) and the provision establishing a fair employment practices commission (Title VII)—would stand as a defeat with the most profound social and political consequences.

The moderate leadership of Roy Wilkins of the NAACP and the Rev. Martin Luther King, Jr. of the Southern Christian Leadership Conference, among others, would be seriously undermined by such a reversal, thereby opening the door for those Negro leaders currently preaching the futility of white man's justice, whether in the courts or in Congress. The related possibility of widespread Negro defections from the Democratic column in the November Presidential election is not lost upon the Texan who will need their votes to ensure his election.

Compromise on other important sections, such as the authority for the Federal Government to intervene in school desegregation suits and other civil rights cases (Titles III and IV), the further protection of voting rights (Title I), and the cut-off of Federal funds from segregated state activities (Title VI), would carry similar risks. In short, the normal complement of expendable items that provide the currency of the legislative process simply is not available to the President under existing circumstances.

Of all recent Presidents, Lyndon Johnson would seem to be the most seriously hobbled by this situation. His ability to hammer out a viable Senate compromise on civil rights was demonstrated in 1957 and again in 1960 when Congress passed legislation designed to protect the voting rights of disfranchised Negroes in the South. On both occasions, however, Johnson became deeply involved in the decision to pluck from the bill those provisions deemed most undesirable by Southern opponents.

In 1957, for example, the historic Title III, permitting the Attorney General to intervene directly to protect an individual's civil rights as guaranteed by the fourteenth Amendment, landed in the discard heap after it had been approved by the House of Representatives. In 1960, the coalition led by Johnson and Senator Everett M. Dirksen, the Republican minority leader, successfully repelled all attempts to provide for Federal voting registrars with authority to register Negro voters in areas where systematic discrimination was discovered. As a substitute the Senate approved the so-called "referee" plan, which directed all voting cases into the courts for time-consuming litigation.

In both instances the proponents of civil rights declared that the legislation passed was fundamentally worthless. The Southerners accepted bills they still disliked but which might have been far more stringent without Johnson's involvement. The majority leader, for his part, took most of the credit for guiding through the Senate the first two civil rights bills in over eighty years. Whether or not the bills would have passed without his willingness to assist in the removal of their most controversial sections is impossible to say. Nevertheless, the importance of his role in reaching these accommodations was clear.

Master of the Political Chess Board

If the passage of legislation consisted in nothing more than determining the lowest common denominator among opposing factions, the outlook for civil rights in 1964 would be bleak indeed. It remains questionable, for example, whether the pro-civil rights forces will be able to produce enough votes (about 66 or 67) to invoke cloture and halt the expected Southern filibuster. (The most optimistic nose count discloses a shortage of 7–8 votes.) Moreover, past efforts to break a filibuster by outlasting the Southerners have always collapsed before the filibuster itself did.

These facts—taken alone—indicate that the legislation will pass the Senate only through compromise of some critical section of the bill such as public accommodations—that is if you follow the "art of the possible" technique used in '57 and '60.

But the actual situation is not that hopeless. Lyndon B. Johnson as President—as distinct from Johnson the majority leader—can be expected to enter the forthcoming fray with a determination quite unlike that which propelled him into the two previous encounters over civil rights. His task as majority leader was to hold together the badly divided Democratic Party and still produce some legislation. His job today is to pass without substantial change the civil rights bill enacted by the House. Johnson cannot afford to rely solely on the device of determining what is "possible" on the basis of criteria supplied by the Southerners.

In the earlier situations the *threat* of a Southern filibuster, tacitly supported by many Republicans and Western Democrats, provided the lever Johnson needed to justify the compromises he claimed were necessary in order to pass the bills. Some persons wondered then, and wonder now, just how potent the filibuster would actually be in a battle to the finish.

Faced with a determined and legislatively skilled President, a team of Senate leaders (Mansfield and Humphrey) committed to passage of the bill in its present form, a well-organized civil rights lobby and a country aware of the stakes involved, the Southern opponents will be dealing with a constellation of forces never before assembled in support of civil rights legislation. Under this combined pressure, the filibuster may reveal itself to be a paper tiger. President Johnson appears ready to find out.

During his years as majority leader Johnson demonstrated a remarkable ability to use every fragment of power and influence he could locate. He knew he lacked the power to command his undisciplined and loosely organized Democratic forces. He could never demand that a Senator do his bidding. Thus his method had to be grounded in personal persuasion and the ability to structure a legislative situation so that a majority of Senators found it in their best interest to follow Johnson's plan of action.

The art of legislative leadership is somewhat analogous to playing chess on a twelve-dimensional chess board. An infinite variety of moves and strategies exist to win the game, and these are in constant and confusing flux. Sometimes a leader can appeal successfully to considerations of party loyalty, or "voting the state's interests," or upholding the dignity of the Senate. At other times a combination of these and other considerations can enlist wavering Senators. Johnson's great (and often misunderstood) ability as majority leader stemmed from his mastery of this twelve-dimensional chess board, i.e., his skill at identifying and executing the complex series of moves that would produce the necessary votes on a given issue.

How did Johnson accomplish those often amazing feats of legislative magic? Principally he sought to involve himself personally in all aspects of the Senate's life, ranging from the daily business on the floor to the constituency relationships of every Senator. He developed a vast fund of knowledge about the many interests and concerns of every member, and this insight produced opportunities for appeals and favors that frequently would transform an opponent into a supporter. "There never was a legislative puzzle that lacked a solution," Johnson would assert, "if only you can locate all the pieces."

LBJ Does Not Intend to Lose

Anyone who blandly suggests that the skills that produced an effective majority leader can be transferred intact to the Presidency fails to appreciate the operational significance of our separated branches of government. Congress, regardless of party control, harbors basic suspicions about the President and the Executive branch, and reacts with an ingrown defensiveness when the gulf between the branches is bridged in too cavalier a fashion. One must, nevertheless, recognize that Johnson's talent for surrounding a member of Congress with a dazzling combination of personal appeals, factors of self-interest, requests for party loyalty and judicious flattery will not totally vanish in his new role as President.

How can Johnson put these skills to work in the present battle for civil rights legislation in the Senate? If the current social and political circumstances suggest the futility of attempting to seek a *modus vivendi* with the bill's opponents, what factors can be used to drum up support among doubtful Senators?

First, Johnson can be expected to attempt to establish in the Senate the amazing bipartisan coalition of Northern Democrats and Republicans that rolled to victory in the House. The outraged cries of Rep. Howard Smith, field general of the Southern forces, when his erstwhile comrade-in-arms Rep. Charles Halleck, the Republican floor leader, jumped on the civil rights bandwagon still echo in the House chamber. Rep. William McCulloch, the ranking Republican member of the Judiciary Committee, and his chief lieutenant, Rep. John Lindsay, never wavered in their support of the legislation. They have, moreover, vehemently announced that the bill's Republican backers will not be parties to any major compromises hatched in the Senate. This raises the possibility of a deadlocked Senate-House conference committee if any serious adjustments are made in the Senate bill.

The strong Republican commitment in the House to preserve the existing bill should significantly increase the pressure on Senate Republicans to invoke cloture or whatever is needed to keep the legislation intact. Senator Dirksen has publicly opposed the public accommodations provision; thus his unqualified support will not be secured easily. Yet his attitude will be the major factor in determining whether or not a bloc of 23–25 Republican votes can be rounded up for cloture. The President, therefore, can be expected to seek ways whereby the House Republicans supporting the bill can bring their full influence to bear on their Senate brethren.

The rare peak of efficiency achieved by the Leadership Conference on Civil Rights, the chief lobbyists for the bill, also places a potent weapon in the President's hands. (The Conference is comprised of about sixty civil rights organizations combined to effect action by the Federal Government at all levels.) The churches in particular have flexed their long-dormant political muscles with surprising effectiveness. It has been informally suggested by Leadership Conference officials that certain key Senators will be targets for "the damndest invasion of ministers, priests and rabbis Washington has ever seen."

Augmenting these pressures will be appeals by the President for party and personal loyalty directed at wavering Western Democrats, full use of his intimate knowledge of the inner workings of Congress, and a display of the Johnson toughness and determination that has become a Washington legend. As the Presidential net closes on those Western Democrats and Republicans who have never supported civil rights legislation, the possibility of invoking cloture will improve.

But even if this combination of Johnsonian power and persuasion does not produce the necessary two-thirds majority, the likelihood of surviving the filibuster increases significantly. Without discussing the complicated parliamentary procedure, it is possible under the Senate rules for the Southerners to exhaust their allotted number of speeches if the Senate remains in session for twelve to fourteen hours each day for approximately ten weeks.

The maintenance of such a killing schedule demands an iron commitment by the Senate leadership to see the issue through without compromise or negotiation. This determination has never existed in any previous civil rights battle, and only the President can supply the pressure to sustain such a commitment. Whatever Lyndon Johnson's strengths and weaknesses as President may be, he is uniquely prepared to do precisely this.

The victory, if it comes, will be largely his; a defeat would also become his personal burden. This is, therefore, one fight Lyndon Johnson does not intend to lose.

THE CRITICAL PHASE IN CIVIL RIGHTS

The expected Southern democratic filibuster against the House-passed civil rights bill began on March 9, 1964 when Majority Leader Mike Mansfield (D., Montana) moved to make it the Senate's pending business. With occasional fits and starts, the filibuster continued through March and April and into May. The troops—both inside and outside the Senate—were getting restless.

This piece suggests how the bipartisan floor managers—Senators Hubert Humphrey (D., Minnesota) and Thomas Kuchel (R., California)—were dealing with these growing pressures. An element of great importance was the romancing of Senator Everett Dirksen (Illinois), the Republican floor leader, to assume the same heroic posture that had been such a critical factor in the Nuclear Test Ban Treaty's overwhelming approval the prior September.

Dirksen viewed himself in heroic terms, linking his oratorical abilities to the great Senate orators of old: Daniel Webster, John C. Calhoun, and Henry Clay. At a more mundane level, he also was the key to the approximately ten Republican senators without whom cloture and the bill's eventual passage was out of reach. Mansfield consulted with Dirksen every day and went out of his way to include him in major decisions. Humphrey focused on public opinion. Following his effusive praise of Dirksen while appearing on a network news interview show during the early stages of the Senate debate, Humphrey responded to my query that "didn't you overdo it a little in praising Dirksen?"

"That is impossible," Humphrey said. "It is not possible to praise Everett to excess. I want to direct the spotlights—the pink lights, the blue lights—on center stage. Sooner or later, Everett will be unable to stand it any longer and he will step into the spotlights. When that happens, John, we will pass the civil rights bill."

It pretty much unfolded the way Humphrey predicted. Only a lot of work was needed to hold things together in the Senate until Dirksen was ready to claim center stage.

THE CRITICAL PHASE IN CIVIL RIGHTS
C&C – May 11, 1964

Can a group of Senators with only a marginal commitment to civil rights provide the extraordinary push that will be needed to get the pending bill through its last critical steps? This is the vexing question confronting Senators Hubert H. Humphrey and Thomas H. Kuchel, bipartisan leaders of the civil rights forces in the Senate.

A substantial majority of their colleagues support the bill's broad objectives but most lack the intense personal involvement found in about a dozen of the Democratic and Republican leaders fighting for the bill, or, for that matter, in about an equal number of the Southern opponents.

Even when these less-involved Senators are willing to join the battle, they do so in the spirit of a volunteer army ready to go AWOL at a moment's notice. Speaking engagements back home lure these troops from the battlefield, making it difficult to produce a quorum without which the Senate must recess and debate flounders.

These Senators are also prey for seductive amendments such as those initially offered by Minority Leader Everett Dirksen. The *quid pro quo* is implicitly clear: accept these amendments and the outlook for cloture will improve greatly. But what if these amendments would also critically weaken sections of the bill—i.e., public accommodations?

Earlier efforts to pass strong civil rights legislation illustrate the problem Humphrey and Kuchel now face. The small band of strongly pro-civil rights Senators entered the fray with banners flying, unbounded enthusiasm and overflowing optimism. The Southern opponents promptly transformed the debate into a filibuster. The remaining Senators—a substantial majority—have generally supported the legislation but with widely varying degrees of commitment. It is no surprise to find many of them prone to early battle fatigue.

Once this feeling has begun to spread, the search for a compromise acceptable to the Southerners and the less-involved Senators has been actively pursued. This has always left just the handful of civil rights supporters to prolong the fight in hopes of winning a stronger bill. It was then only a matter of time until the accommodation was reached and a badly weakened bill passed.

A repetition of this process is precisely what Humphrey and Kuchel have sought to avoid at all costs; this is what President Johnson has informed them must not take place. How, then, are they to maintain the commitment needed to defeat a filibuster among Senators from states where the civil rights revolution is hardly an issue? How is such a Senator persuaded to continue making the personal sacrifices required, such as driving to the Senate at 1:00A.M., to answer a quorum call?

One approach is to encourage the belief among Senators that the legislation is predestined to pass, that President Johnson won't let Congress relax until the civil rights bill has been delivered to his desk, and that the Southern opposition is steadily crumbling. Foot soldiers are much less likely to desert a winning army.

In that respect Senator Dirksen's willingness to work with the bipartisan leadership in proposing the substitute jury trial amendment was particularly significant. Every Senator, especially those from the South, knows that Dirksen holds the balance of power on the bill; his decision to join with the civil rights forces, even on this amendment of marginal importance, provided Humphrey and Kuchel with a valuable boost at a critical phase in the battle. It also provided an opportunity to rally the troops for the final drive for passage.

Humphrey and Kuchel know that this drive must be planned with great precision so that forces inside and outside the Senate advocating a strong bill can sustain the additional pressure against the filibuster without opening the bill to unacceptable compromises.

Daily sessions need to be lengthened to fifteen or sixteen hours, and then to twenty-four hours. Rules controlling the conduct of debate must be rigidly enforced at all times. Quorum calls must be answered at any time, day or night. Outside groups must bring appropriate pressure to bear on specific Senators whose votes are needed for cloture. This can probably produce the 65–67 votes for cloture and avoid serious damage to the bill.

But it is a delicate and essentially unpredictable operation. The temptation to dispense with the battle by major compromises grows in direct proportion to personal frustration and inconvenience. To forestall such a catastrophe, the leaders working for a strong bill will have to draw upon every available resource, particularly the telephone and strong right arm of Lyndon B. Johnson.

In sum, the civil rights bill now enters its most critical phase with pitfalls on every hand.

HOW THE BILL WAS PASSED

This summary of how the civil rights bill was passed still rings true four decades later. Not included in this analysis are these personal recollections from the climactic days of the great struggle:

- Senator Richard Russell of Georgia, the *generalissimo* of the Southern opposition, railing against the flood of "priests, rabbis, bishops, ministers, deacons, pastors, and stated clerks" who descended on Washington to lobby for passage. Russell went on to observe that " . . . the philosophy of coercion by the men of the cloth in this case is the same doctrine that dictated the acts of Torquemada in the infamous days of the Spanish Inquisition." While Russell never went on to explain exactly what he had in mind (thumbscrews? the rack?), the statement suggests that the forces of organized mainline religion had indeed made a difference—perhaps the decisive difference—in lining up conservative Republican votes.

- Senator Everett Dirksen, his mellifluous voice booming and his unkempt white hair tossing, concluding the debate just prior to the vote on final passage: "But standing on the pinnacle of this night, looking back, looking around, looking forward . . . this is 'the year that was,' and it will be so recorded by the bone pickers who somehow put together all the items that portray man's journey through time that is history. I am prepared for the vote!" Dirksen had, at long last, stepped into the spotlight and claimed center stage. As

Humphrey predicted, the result was decisive—final passage by the count of 73–27.

- Having dinner that historic evening of final passage (June 19, 1964) with Humphrey at Paul Young's Restaurant on Connecticut Avenue, only to learn half way through dinner that Senator Ted Kennedy and Senator Birch Bayh had crashed in a light plane. Their fate was not known and we feared the worst. Our dinner limped to a conclusion. This frightening event further underscored in Humphrey's mind his worry and concern over his son, Bob, who had been diagnosed several days earlier with lymphatic cancer in his neck. Bob and Mrs. Humphrey were in Minnesota but Humphrey felt he had no choice but to remain on the front lines in Washington. It was an agonizing decision for a father to make and the strain and worry were clearly evident during the final several days. Bob, it can be reported, made a full recovery. And Ted Kennedy and Birch Bayh survived the plane crash.

- Leaving the Senate wing of the Capitol with Humphrey a couple of hours after final passage, and encountering a crowd of several hundred people who were just standing there, waiting to thank the senators as they left. When Humphrey appeared, the crowd burst into applause and cheering, young and old, white and black, jumping up and down. Moses had arrived. Humphrey just beamed from ear to ear and charged into the crowd to thank the celebrants. Being Humphrey, he also seized the occasion to shout triumphant words across the excited crowd. When can you last recall a crowd of people spontaneously waiting at the U.S. Capitol for hours to thank their representatives for doing something good? It was a moment that made you feel, deep in your heart, that democracy, informed by justice, would prevail. A rare moment, indeed, these days.

HOW THE BILL WAS PASSED
C&C – July 10, 1964

Any Congressional decision to pass a bill is a compound of many factors—legislative strategy, political pressure, personalities, public opinion, good fortune and personal beliefs. The key to victory in a legislative struggle is the ability to identify and combine the factors that, in a given set of circumstances, will produce the required margin of support. This is never an easy operation.

The Senate has been known as the graveyard for civil rights legislation: one need only count the tombstones to verify the legitimacy of this reputation. A simple majority of Senators is never sufficient to pass a meaningful civil rights bill because two-thirds are needed first to break the inevitable Southern filibuster. Due to this crucial difference from normal procedures, there has always seemed to be no more impossible task than passing a strong civil rights bill.

How, then, were the lessons of history defied and the tables turned on the previously unbeatable Southern caucus? What unique combination of factors was responsible for the stunning victory?

First, the House of Representatives took the essential step of passing an effective and comprehensive bill through the efforts of a truly bipartisan coalition. The fact that 78 percent of the Republicans supported the bill could not be ignored by their brethren in the Senate (e.g., the entire Illinois delegation voted for the bill—an item of some interest to Senator Dirksen), and Republican votes spelled the difference between defeat and victory.

The bipartisan House leadership also served notice on the Senate leaders that any crippling amendments would not be acceptable and would place the whole bill in jeopardy. In short, there could be no repetition of the events that took place in 1957 and 1960 when the Senate deleted principal features of the House bills and then forced the House to accept their changes.

Second, the bill's bipartisan supporters in the Senate commanded by Senators Humphrey and Kuchel were carefully organized to withstand the rigors of the protracted Southern filibuster. In prior battles the civil rights advocates resembled a band of disorganized irregulars as compared to the disciplined and well-drilled Southern shock troops. In 1964, however, they failed to produce a quorum on only one occasion (out of nearly 200 quorum calls) and were never caught unprepared or outmaneuvered by the fabled Southern tacticians. The active support of the President and the Senate majority leader—factors not present in the '57 and '60 struggles—also sustained the bill's proponents during the longest filibuster in Senate history.

Third, the chief Southern strategist, Senator Russell, underrated the skill and determination of the civil rights forces inside and outside the Senate, misunderstood the degree of national support for the legislation, and misjudged the likelihood that Senator Dirksen would become an outspoken proponent of cloture and a strong bill. Russell based his campaign of massive resistance, i.e., preventing votes on all significant amendments during the two months preceding cloture, on the mistaken belief that the initial attempts to invoke cloture would fail. Then, Russell theorized, the bill would become highly vulnerable to emasculating amendments as the price for winning additional cloture votes. And the stage would be set for a Senate–House deadlock in the conference committee.

The civil rights leaders meanwhile decided not to attempt cloture until they were sure of victory. When Russell failed to win the first battle of cloture on June 10, he simultaneously lost all opportunity to significantly weaken the bill.

If, however, Russell had permitted an occasional vote on selected amendments—those directed principally against the public accommodations and equal employment opportunity titles—it is quite likely that the measure would have been fundamentally impaired. Russell's reliance solely on the filibuster helped to drive Humphrey and Dirksen into an alliance that totally routed the Southern and reactionary Republican forces.

Fourth, the outside forces supporting the bill conducted themselves with amazing restraint and effectiveness. The absence of massive demonstrations in Washington denied many Senators an excuse to oppose cloture and the bill because of "outside pressure and coercion." The activities of the Leadership Conference on Civil Rights and the religious groups in Midwestern states where Republican Senators were wavering, e.g., Iowa, Nebraska, South Dakota, Idaho and Illinois, produced constituent pressures normally unavailable to Democratic Congressional leaders.

Finally, the Dirksen-Humphrey alliance was the crucial ingredient that produced the winning formula. The forging of this partnership and the creation of the Dirksen-Humphrey substitute bill—a dual operation that required unusual patience, determination and good faith on all sides—guaranteed the votes that made cloture a reality and insured passage of the most significant piece of social legislation in thirty years.

THE PROPER ROLE OF GOVERNMENT:
A Critique of Senator Goldwater's Views

With nearly forty years of hindsight to illuminate the scene, the presidential candidacy of Barry Goldwater in 1964 can be viewed in many lights. From one perspective, it was the beginning of a conservative tide in American politics that swept Reagan, Bush the father, and Bush the son to victory, twice, and continues to grow. From another perspective, Goldwater's crushing defeat by Lyndon Johnson ushered in the Great Society and its remarkable record of domestic achievement, clearing the activist agenda of most items that had been pending for years. It served as the bridge to the Promised Land. From yet another, it signaled the demise of moderate Republicanism that had controlled the party since Dewey and Eisenhower and had recently played such a decisive role in enacting the civil rights bill. And, as predicted by Johnson, the Southern electorate swung inexorably away from the Democrats into a newly invigorated conservative Republican Party.

Writing during the presidential campaign of 1964 (when I also was part of Senator Humphrey's vice presidential campaign), I had a more limited and focused perspective: What kind of president would Goldwater make?

It is evident that I approached this assignment while still in recovery from my graduate school studies at the University of Chicago. The words have that smarty-pants graduate school ring to them. This is not to say that I disagree today with the points I made in 1964. Not at all, I think I made some sense—only I could have done it without sounding quite so stuffy. It also turns out that I wrote a critique that, in many ways, can be directed toward George W. Bush and his approach to the presidency and the governing of America. Who could have imagined?

Nancy and I will always remember Goldwater from the perspective of the Atlantic City billboard caper that we witnessed firsthand. As delegates and others at the 1964 Democratic National Convention in Atlantic City left Convention Hall to stroll along the boardwalk, we encountered an enormous full-color billboard of Barry Goldwater looking heroically down upon us, along with the legend, "In Your Heart You Know He's Right." We couldn't avoid looking at the billboard several times a day and it became very annoying. Democratic activists do not appreciate being lectured to by an archconservative Republican—even if it was from a height of fifty feet.

Our good friend, Stan Frankel, did more than just grumble. He acted. Stan arranged for an adventurous soul to climb up the billboard in the middle of the night and affix an additional message: "Yes, FAR right!" So now the message read: "In Your Heart You Know He's Right . . . Yes, FAR right!" The wire services transmitted a photo of the retouched billboard around the country and we all felt a lot better. I always suspected that Stan Frankel, an accomplished businessman, political activist, and good friend, got a greater kick out of his Atlantic City billboard caper than many of his more substantive achievements.

The ultimate irony concerning Barry Goldwater is that he became a far less ideological figure as he grew older, much more attractive to persons of all persuasions, and totally unpredictable when it came to speaking out on current issues. When he finally left the Senate in 1986, there was scarcely a senator who didn't consider him a friend.

A CRITIQUE OF SENATOR GOLDWATER'S VIEWS
The Proper Role of Government
C&C – October 5, 1964

BARRY GOLDWATER stands today as the most principled man in American politics. And it is precisely this almost total reliance upon a litany of principles—useful in all situations and conditions—that makes Senator Goldwater's candidacy for President so disturbing.

He and his more committed supporters revel in the fact that his popularity is rooted in the public's growing appreciation of a man of principle. Such a man apparently scorns political expediency in his passion to uphold certain fundamental tenets of natural law and government in the conduct of our domestic affairs. Yet even a cursory examination of Mr. Goldwater's writings and political record demonstrates that this steadfast reliance upon principle has served perhaps to disqualify him for the American Presidency, rather than prepare him for it.

Any political decision reflects certain presuppositions about the nature of man and the proper role of government in human affairs. Although in American politics it is rarely necessary to express these presuppositions explicitly, there are legitimate differences of opinion that can be profitably examined and debated. The Republican nominee may offer this country such an opportunity.

But all self-proclaimed spokesmen of political morality face one special requirement: that their preaching provide a recognizable basis for making workable decisions in terms of the daily tasks of government. To a large degree the major contributors to American political thought have been persons charged with making the practical operating decisions.

Unlike the Founding Fathers, whose notions of political right were matched by their political accomplishment, Mr. Goldwater has never had any direct or personal responsibility for translating his vibrant generalities into less scintillating specifics. In fact, his preoccupation with principles has provided him instead with a means of avoiding the agonizing task of reaching policy decisions that the real world must accept.

All Vision, No Program

We find Mr. Goldwater's writings and speeches sprinkled liberally with declamations about freedom, balancing order with liberty, stimulating the development of the whole man, and the need to resist concentrations of public authority. He sees politics as "the art of achieving the maximum amount of freedom for individuals that is consistent with the maintenance of the social order."

These notions of natural law serve to project an image of a man sorely dissatisfied with the existing state of affairs, prepared to remove the burden of government involvement from many areas of life, and calling upon his fellow citizens to join him in this crusade for individualism and self-responsibility. A return to conservative principles is the key to national salvation.

This preoccupation with principles manifested itself in the Senator's attempt to abolish the traditional party platform in favor of a statement of principles. If the Republican Party had adopted the suggestion, the American electorate would probably have received something similar to his recent testimony before the Republican Platform Committee, e.g., "Let us dedicate ourselves to strengthening government in its proper spheres and at its proper levels while withdrawing government from needless and damaging intervention." Or: "In the conduct of its monetary and fiscal affairs, our government must above all replace capricious and predatory schemes with consistent and predictable policies." A collection of these exhortations—and nothing more—would have made the promise of a "choice not an echo" quite difficult to fulfill.

It would be unfair to say that Mr. Goldwater completely fails to appreciate the need for some specificity in these matters of principle. Both *The Conscience of a Conservative* and his more recent book, *Where I Stand,* are billed as attempts "to show the connection between conservative principles so widely espoused and conservative action so generally neglected." Yet a careful reading of the sections devoted to particular policy areas discloses no comprehensive program of action capable of bringing his conservative vision to life.

For example, on fiscal responsibility the Senator observes:

> The first fiscal responsibility of government is to preserve the value of the dollar. It can do this by prudent budgeting, by living within the means of the people who pay the bills, and by encouraging individual initiative.

On labor-management relations:

> To achieve industrial peace, we must maintain a balance among the rights of employees, employers and the public. The balance is best assured when laws are clear and fairly administered, and when government does not inject itself in a partisan way into dealings between employers and employees.

Other examples could be cited from the sections on federalism, states' rights, civil rights, social security and the TVA. In only one area—support for education—does he make some truly specific suggestions for policy alternatives, i.e., tax credits to local taxpayers, to persons supporting students at an accredited college or university, and for persons making gifts to colleges or universities. Although one can dispute the merits of such a proposal, at least it contains certain recognizable policy alternatives to ponder and evaluate.

The Avoidance of Policy-making

One fundamental fact seems clear in Mr. Goldwater's writings: he is most hesitant to move beyond the realm of generalization into the more unpleasant world of specifics—where decisions tend to be a mixture of the desirable and the undesirable. But it is in this latter world that the President must reside.

In his numerous speeches, the problem of specificity is less acute. We discover a variety of suggestions, e.g., making social security voluntary, withdrawing the Federal Government from welfare programs, decreasing government spending, and advocating right-to-work laws. Yet these suggestions appear to be largely rhetorical devices; seldom, if ever, does he provide a comprehensive and logical program to accomplish these objectives of lessening the role of government in human affairs.

During his twelve years in the Senate Mr. Goldwater has avoided being placed in the position where the burden of political decision rested on his shoulders. Who can recall any major piece of legislation—or even an amendment—that he seriously advanced during this period? Despite the Democratic majority for ten of these twelve years, other Republicans managed to participate actively in the process of hammering out viable legislation.

Or who can recall the Senator debating the substance of a pending measure, thereby demonstrating in even a single specific area the depth of understanding we expect the President to possess in many areas? How then did Mr. Goldwater spend his twelve-year tenure as a Senator? Quite simply: he delivered thousands of speeches to discontented audiences on the need to return the tested and true principles of conservatism to our councils of government.

The issue of extremism in politics clearly has its roots in the Arizonan's preoccupation with principles and his avoidance of policy-making responsibilities. When he deliberately underlined the two famous sentences of his acceptance speech, i.e., "Extremism in the defense of liberty is no vice. Moderation in the pursuit of justice is no virtue," he was acting as a man used to the luxury of speaking in extreme terms. But a President seldom enjoys this luxury.

If a President is to retain the confidence of the nation, his actions must win the consent of widely differing interests in this country and abroad. For the President extremism is suicide; moderation is salvation.

Likewise Mr. Goldwater's reputation for speaking first and thinking later is the predictable result of a political diet that for twelve years has avoided the indigestible lumps of political decisions for the Pablum of generalities.

It is, therefore, most difficult to reach any final conclusions about the probable impact of the Senator's principles on the conduct of our government. His proclamations about the need to "maximize free-dom," "balance order with liberty," etc. offer few hints about how a Goldwater administration would actually come to grips with the dif-ficult and complex issues no President can avoid.

"Ever-Eager Fingers of Bureaucracy"

One could also express a certain disquiet over his apparent lack of comprehension of the existing mechanisms of the American govern-mental system. No single administration—however determined—can remake this system; it would appear to be desirable for the potential President to demonstrate a working knowledge of it.

Mr. Goldwater's writings deal particularly with the question of states' rights and federalism. In *Where I Stand* he notes that states' rights is "a check on the steady accumulation of massive power in the hands of national bureaucrats." He continues:

> . . . The states can fit their powers and programs to the varied needs of their people. It is in the cities and towns, and in person-to-person relationships, that their immediate needs arise. And it is there—certainly

not in Washington, D. C.—that public servants can
best adapt governmental power to the individual
human situation.

Speaking before the National Association of Counties, Senator
Goldwater trotted out certain variations of this theme. He talked of
"Washington's ever-eager fingers of bureaucracy," and he castigated
the Federal Government as "obsessed by the enlargement of its role
and its personnel."

This conception of battered and defenseless state and local governments cowering before a predatory Federal Government is a difficult
one to accept in light of the facts. In recent years expansion of
American government has taken place primarily at the state and local
levels. (For example, since 1946 the number of Federal civilian
employees has declined about 10 percent—while the number of state
and local employees has risen by over 100 percent. The Federal debt
has risen by slightly more than 10 percent in the past eighteen years;
state and local debt has climbed by over 400 percent.)

Mr. Goldwater also failed to acknowledge another basic fact about
the operation of our Federal system: Federal agencies have devolved
an immense amount of decision-making to their state and regional
offices, which are generally staffed by local people. Federal programs
are run on terms highly favorable to states and localities: the Federal
Government provides a major portion of the money, requires certain
minimum standards, and leaves the implementation of the program to
the wisdom and abilities of local officials. This arrangement would
appear to balance states' rights with states' responsibilities in a reasonably equitable manner.

In his address to the county officials Mr. Goldwater recommended
a comprehensive review of Federal grant-in-aid practices. Again the
Senator apparently was unaware that this question does receive intensive analysis by the Commission on Intergovernmental Relations, a body

established by Congress in 1959. Moreover, a Senate subcommittee has been investigating this same question during the 88th Congress.

Mr. Goldwater also speaks frequently of the need to "return" certain governmental functions to the states, thereby saving the "freight charges" incurred by collecting the tax revenues in Washington and then redistributing them among the states in the form of Federally sponsored programs. In fact, few states—if any—have the slightest desire to assume complete responsibility for programs in which they participate with the Federal Government.

The Federal-State Action Committee, established during the Eisenhower administration, labored for two years to discover programs that could be "returned" to the states. A minor vocational education program was readied for shipment back to the states, but the effort collapsed. Why? The states refused to accept the program, even when alternative revenue sources had been provided. Governors—if not Senator Goldwater—realized that continued Federal participation was an essential ingredient in the success of the program.

It is hardly original to describe Mr. Goldwater as the only candidate running backwards into the twentieth century. Yet it is disturbing to discover his apparent lack of understanding and information about certain basic operating realities of our system of government. In any intelligent discussion of this matter, one fact stands out above all others: the respective levels of government are partners in a common enterprise. These governments are collaborators—not antagonists— and he who fails to understand this is indeed out of touch with the contemporary situation.

My concern with Senator Goldwater is not with his addiction to certain abstract principles—with which many persons would probably agree—but rather with the quality of decisions he would render as President when specifics could no longer be avoided. His meager record as an elected public official gives little basis for assurance. This concern is compounded by his apparent lack of a working understanding of the dynamics of American government in the twentieth century. The combination of these two factors can only raise the gravest doubts about his qualifications for the most demanding job in the world.

BUILDING THE GREAT SOCIETY, LBJ STYLE

Nicholas D. Picque (NDP) made his initial appearance in this article on the outlook for Lyndon Johnson's legislative program in the aftermath of the 1964 landslide. Since I was now working on Vice President Humphrey's staff, I concluded some protective cover was appropriate for all concerned parties. Folks were more relaxed in those days, one can say in retrospect. I informed the Vice President about this somewhat unorthodox scheme. He said it sounded just fine to him. He also noted that *C&C* was an outstanding journal, started by his good friend Reinhold Niebuhr and "worthy of my efforts." For some reason, I can't envision Vice President Cheney having a comparable response.

My comments about LBJ's leadership style, all drawn from my emerging dissertation on the Senate majority leader, were largely on target. But my description of Johnson as a "plodder in the formulation of national policies and programs" could not have been more off the mark. The year of 1965 exploded into a period of legislative accomplishment unseen since FDR's initial "100 Days" in the spring of 1933. LBJ relished the growing comparisons with his idol and mentor, Franklin Roosevelt.

A generation of stalled Democratic proposals—from Medicare to Federal aid to education, with many others in between—all came to fruition in this one extraordinary outburst of presidential initiative and positive congressional response. No "Deadlock on the Potomac" this congressional session. The Promised Land finally had been reached. Unforeseen at the time I wrote this article, but ultimately one of Johnson's greatest achievements, was passage of the Voting Rights

Act of 1965. Passed in response to the brutal attacks on Rev. Martin Luther King, Jr., and his Southern Christian Leadership Conference supporters in Selma, Alabama, the Voting Rights Act finally put in place the Federal legal structure that made voting a reality for African-Americans and other minorities across the South and elsewhere where patterns of voting inequality existed. From Johnson's perspective, it closed the circle that began with enactment of the Civil Rights Act of 1957, the first tentative steps to secure voting rights for racial minorities.

In this article I ask the question whether Lyndon Johnson possesses " . . . the vision and courage to make a great President?" Looking at his domestic legislative record of 1965, it would be impossible to withhold a resounding affirmative response to this question. We truly believed that liberal democracy was on the march. Old evils and difficulties were being attacked directly. The national consensus for action ensured victory. It was an extraordinary and exhilarating time to be working in Washington.

But lurking in the shadows, largely unseen and unappreciated by most of us, was the nation's deepening involvement in the swamp of Vietnam. Within a year, the troop buildups had begun in earnest. Demonstrators against the war were raising their voices and building momentum.

Johnson's great national consensus for domestic achievement was shattered, never to be revived.

BUILDING THE GREAT SOCIETY, LBJ STYLE

NICHOLAS D. PICQUE

C&C – January 11, 1965

THOSE PERSONS expecting the Great Society to be launched according to some grand design—set forth presumably in the Inaugural Address or State of the Union message—are likely to be disappointed. Lyndon Johnson's Great Society, like Carl Sandburg's fog, will probably creep in upon us slowly and quietly. Rarely will we be treated to thunderclaps or lightning bolts.

Washington is, to be sure, busy enough these days. The President is conferring. Task forces are reporting. The Vice-President-elect is coordinating. And certain members of Congress are drumming up support for themselves as new Congressional leaders or for proposals to modernize Congressional machinery.

Yet this activity lacks the urgent enthusiasm or confident idealism that characterized the opening months of the Kennedy Administration. It's been ages since anyone even mentioned a "crusade." So it is not surprising that critics are already beginning to ask aloud whether Lyndon Johnson is capable of supplying the necessary substance and commitment to flesh out his skeletal vision of the Great Society.

John F. Kennedy considered the spoken and written word to be a principal resource of the Presidency. He labored over his major public utterances. He bombarded Congress with special messages on a wide variety of topics. He actively sought to challenge and inspire both public officials and private citizens. And in so doing Kennedy produced—especially prior to the Bay of Pigs—a remarkable sense of excitement and commitment throughout the Federal establishment.

The Policy Process Is Evolutionary

Lyndon Johnson, by comparison, appears to be almost a plodder in the formulation of national policies and programs. He locks up the task force reports. He procrastinates on vital Federal appointments. He rarely misses an opportunity to dismiss the significance of the size of his election victory, explaining that it certainly did not constitute a mandate for dramatic innovation in national policies. It is surprising that few persons have been stirred to their depths over the challenge of building the Great Society.

It is essential to understand that President Johnson's years of service on Capitol Hill established the view that meaningful national programs are seldom produced through sudden inspiration or dramatic bursts of activity, however exciting or stimulating this might be. He sees the policy process as more evolutionary—as characterized by give-and-take, mutual accommodation and patience. He believes this process cannot be hurried unduly given the pluralistic nature of American society and the decentralization of political power in this country.

Lyndon Johnson, moreover, prefers to operate on the inside: that is, he wants to deal directly with the Congressional chieftains, agency heads, labor and business leaders, and others who possess the leverage to advance or retard his objectives. This approach downgrades the importance of ringing public addresses and eloquent messages to Congress in promoting the Administration's program.

Johnson always attempted to operate on the inside during his tenure as Senate Majority Leader. He made a point of speaking daily to every Democratic Senator. But he also made sure he did it one by one—Senator by Senator. Certain liberal Democrats became distressed over this procedure. They demanded more frequent party caucuses to debate pending legislation and to reach party positions. But Johnson could never quite fathom the thought processes of his liberal brethren: why convene the Democrats and provide an opportunity to disagree openly among themselves? So, few caucuses were held. The reins of power remained firmly in Johnson's hands.

Given Johnson's evolutionary view of policy formation and his reliance upon inside operations, to worry about how the President interprets his "mandate" from the electorate is irrelevant. Mandates as such are important to those Presidents who follow a more public—or outside—course of action, or who are planning radical departures in policy. Even if his victory over Goldwater had been narrow, it seems unlikely that President Johnson would have altered in any significant way existing plans to develop and promote the policies of the Great Society.

Working With Congress

But what about Congress? Surely a net gain of thirty-eight Democrats in the House and two in the Senate (producing Democratic majorities of 295–140 and 66–34) provides a basis for dramatic new initiatives from the Executive branch. Yet Johnson recalls that in 1937 an even larger majority rebelled against Franklin D. Roosevelt (fresh from an even more impressive "mandate") when the President cast covetous eyes on the Supreme Court. Johnson has no intention of emulating his political idol in this respect. There will be no legislative bombshells coming from the White House in 1965.

Nor does the President intend to permit his Administration—at any level—to take Congress for granted. The word has been passed to the Executive agencies that good Congressional relations is a principal—and personal—responsibility of every Cabinet officer and agency head. The post of Congressional liaison officer has been designated by the President as the second most important position in every agency.

Johnson also recognizes that he faces something of a crisis in leadership on Capitol Hill, especially in the Senate. The elevation of Hubert H. Humphrey, Assistant Majority Leader, to the presiding officer's chair has produced a three-way scramble among Russell Long (La.), Mike Monroney (Okla.) and John Pastore (R. I.) to become the new Democratic whip. At this writing Long (who voted against such priority Administration measures as the civil rights bill, the test-ban treaty, foreign aid and Medicare) holds a commanding lead, primarily due to his dogged and unabashed pursuit of votes. But even if Long is ultimately defeated, Monroney lacks the sense of personal commitment and the spark—so abundantly present in Humphrey—to offset Majority Leader Mansfield's often uninspired and unimaginative leadership. Pastore's weakness lies in the opposite direction; his volatile temper and quick tongue constantly threaten to alienate Senators unnecessarily.

It is interesting to speculate on the extent to which Humphrey will continue to assume some legislative responsibilities for the President. The lessons of history are clear: Vice Presidents had better mind their manners; they venture beyond the sanctuary of the dais at their own risk. But then history has never installed as President and Vice President two such legislative operators as Johnson and Humphrey.

Mechanic or Master Designer?

Considering these factors, what is likely to happen during the early months of the new Administration? First, we can look for concerted efforts to pass legislation left from the last Congress—Medicare, area redevelopment amendments and the Appalachia development bill. Second, we can expect the Administration to continue the process of formulating more specific recommendations in areas of critical domestic need, particularly education and urban development. Third, we can expect vigorous efforts to establish effective procedures to implement the major legislative accomplishments of last year—the civil rights and anti-poverty programs.

This drive to tidy up loose ends and secure effective administration of existing programs will excite few persons inside or outside Washington. Yet it possesses the principal virtue of providing a solid base for subsequent recommendations and accomplishments. In particular, passage of the Medicare bill before Easter would constitute a major substantive victory; it would also demonstrate to Congress that Johnson intends to keep winning the big ones. One fact is clear: the President means to start building in Congress as early as possible the momentum that produced such a magnificent record last year. And this is done by winning every time out.

Yet these early victories, however satisfying in their own right, will provide few clues to the puzzle—does Johnson's approach to the policy process have the capacity to produce decisions that make sense in the long run? As Majority Leader and as President, he left little doubt about his ability as a mechanic. For six years he oiled the Senate's creaking joints; last year he manipulated Congress to enact almost the entire Kennedy legislative program. But how will he do as master designer and planner?

An important clue will be uncovered when Johnson determines the specifics of his education program. The President has already announced his intention to make massive investments in the educational resources of the country. But will he also face up to the major challenge of providing general assistance to elementary and secondary schools including funds for school construction and teachers' salaries? Can he devise an approach that is both constitutional and politically viable? In short, can he resolve the impasse between the Roman Catholic bishops and the National Education Association?

There are, of course, other worthwhile education programs that could be recommended in lieu of general aid such as assistance to the culturally deprived, teacher training and enrichment, and Federally supported research into the process of learning. But this stark fact remains: a decision to postpone again some form of general Federal assistance in favor of increased support for a hodgepodge of subsidiary programs will reveal a disturbing failure of nerve at the highest levels of the Administration.

Lyndon B. Johnson will go about building the Great Society in his own way. He will not be stampeded. He will exhibit his own style and impose his own sense of timing. And it will not disturb him one bit if everything is not accomplished in the first 100 days.

But does the President also perceive fully the dimensions of the tasks that await in the areas of housing, urban development, economic growth and unemployment, education, civil rights and the war on poverty? Is he truly prepared to make the political sacrifices necessary to accomplish these tasks? In short, does he possess the vision and courage to make a great President?

It is impossible to answer these questions at this juncture. But the time for answers will come. And they will be rendered on the basis of hard evidence —pupils educated, houses built, ghettos destroyed, jobs created and Negroes voting.

Thus whatever his timing, whatever his style, Lyndon Johnson cannot avoid indefinitely his time of accounting.

FEDERAL INITIATIVE IN CIVIL RIGHTS:
Bringing the Sleeping Giant of Federal Power to Life

This article anticipated many of the difficulties that were to grip the civil rights struggle in the aftermath of the historically successful enactment of the Civil Rights Act of 1964 and the Voting Rights Act of 1965—such events as urban riots of Detroit and Watts, the rupture with Lyndon Johnson over the issue of Vietnam, the rise of the Black Panthers and other "Black power" advocates, the fiasco of Resurrection City on the Washington Mall, the perceived failure of non-violence, the assassination of Martin Luther King, Jr., and the subsequent rioting in Washington, D.C. and elsewhere. Nicholas D. Picque, bless him, had it exactly right when he wrote about the growing fragmentation of the civil rights forces and the assumption that somehow the Federal government would necessarily be in the middle of all subsequent efforts to conquer the nation's remaining social and economic injustices based on race.

This fragmentation, often bitter, among the civil rights leadership was never more evident than on one pleasant evening in the spring of 1965 while Vice President Humphrey and the nation's civil rights leaders cruised down the Potomac River on a presidential yacht. Humphrey had been tapped by Lyndon Johnson to coordinate the Federal government's massive new civil rights authority. The mechanism for coordination was to be the President's Council on Equal Opportunity, as noted in NDP's article. Wiley Branton, the well-known attorney who had represented the high school students in the Little Rock desegregation case during the Eisenhower administration, was hired as the Council's executive director. I was to follow things from the V.P.'s office.

In these circumstances, it was deemed appropriate for Humphrey to requisition a presidential yacht and invite the civil rights leadership to join him for dinner and discussion. All the major leaders accepted: Martin Luther King, Jr., Roy Wilkins, Whitney Young, Jr., James Farmer, Clarence Mitchell, Andrew Young, Walter Fauntroy, Floyd McKissick, among others. Drinks and dinner were served. Discussion ensued, along with more drinks. In several instances, more than a few drinks were served. All at once, harsh words were exchanged by several of the guests. One of the leaders took a wild swing at another. Pushing, shoving, and cursing ensued.

The Secret Service came running and separated the combatants. Humphrey looked at me, horrified, and his face told the story: What in heaven's name is going on? How could a pleasant evening of cruising, dinner, and discussion turn into a fist fight among some of the nation's most respected civil rights leaders? Although peace was quickly restored, the event, more than we realized at the time, foreshadowed the internal difficulties and struggles that have characterized the civil rights movement to this day (witness the bitter divisions over the issue of "reparations" for slavery).

This ugly incident also foretold the fate of Humphrey as the government's civil rights czar. The notion of the Vice President's office and staff serving as the focal point for civil rights enforcement and implementation was more than presidential assistants in the White House could stomach. Joe Califano, LBJ's principal assistant on domestic issues, quickly arranged to have the President's Council on Equal Opportunity abolished and its duties transferred back to the White House. Humphrey's appeals to LBJ to stop Califano's highjacking fell on deaf ears. Too bad, said Califano, in so many words; I'm running things now. And indeed he was.

But even Califano, with all his presidential leverage, could not avert the growing troubles that transformed the elation of victory following the great legislative victories of 1964 and 1965 into a seemingly never-ending succession of shortfalls, disappointments, and tragedies.

BRINGING THE SLEEPING GIANT OF FEDERAL POWER TO LIFE
Federal Initiative in Civil Rights

NICHOLAS D. PICQUE

C&C – May 3, 1965

OVER THE past several years the growing dynamism of the civil rights movement has been channeled into a series of short-term, relatively manageable operations. Beginning with the March on Washington in 1963, such events as the consideration of the Civil Rights Bill, the Mississippi Summer Project, the challenge by the Mississippi Freedom Democratic Party (MFDP) at the Democratic National Convention, the Presidential election and, currently, the consideration of the Voting Rights Bill in Congress have provided a variety of meaningful outlets for the energies and ambitions of civil rights leaders and their followers.

This series of events produced a substantial degree of unity and common purpose among the civil rights organizations; a willingness existed to initiate projects that would produce results in the foreseeable future. And these activities commanded national attention and participation. The March on Washington, for example, wiped out scheduled TV programing for hours. The testimony by the MFDP before the credentials committee at the Democratic National Convention—again on national TV—provided the only real drama at Atlantic City.

Events at Selma and President Johnson's submission of the Voting Rights Bill may well represent the concluding phase in this period of the civil rights struggle. It seems probable that we are now entering a less ordered and controlled period—one characterized by fragmentation rather than unity and producing a wide variety of local efforts directed at longer range, more complex and less achievable goals.

One basic rationale for passage of the Civil Rights Act of 1964, and the pending Voting Rights Bill, has been the desire to "get the conflicts out of the streets and into the courts." Advocates of this theory point to the cessation of sit-ins and freedom rides as soon as the right of equal access to places of public accommodation had been established. "Remedy the evil," Attorney General Nicholas Katzenbach has observed, "and the danger of violence and public disorder will be largely over."

New Occasions Produce New Violence

But what has happened? Negroes who earlier would have participated in sit-ins to protest segregated lunch counters now have turned their energies toward discrimination in registration and voting. Thus a bloody Sunday afternoon in Selma was just a matter of time.

The Voting Rights Act of 1965 will provide the muscle to eliminate the remaining hard-core areas of voting discrimination in the South. But will this ensure domestic tranquility any more successfully than public accommodations provisions enacted less than a year ago? Far more likely is the prospect that those persons who are fighting Sheriff Jim Clark today will try to run him out of office tomorrow— and this could get very nasty.

Bayard Rustin, in a recent address to the national convention of Americans for Democratic Action, stressed that civil rights demonstrations had served their purpose—that now the Negro should begin the far more difficult task of achieving full political, economic and social equality in both North and South. Rustin is one of the wisest and most effective Negro leaders—he does not make such pronouncements lightly.

Assuming that Rustin's advice is followed, the ending of demonstrations should not suggest that we are beyond hard, painful decisions on civil rights. Indeed, demonstrations themselves absorbed large amounts of frustration and bitterness by providing a nonviolent outlet for the restless activists in the movement. Without an acceptable channel for expressing these frustrations, the potentiality for truly serious racial conflicts is likely to increase.

The Negro in the South will be seeking to implement the Voting Rights Act as a step toward a thorough revamping of the local Southern power structures, especially in areas of heavy Negro concentration. (Incidentally, the bill should pass Congress in a form somewhat stronger than that recommended initially by President Johnson.) In the process, pockets of last-ditch resistance and terrorism could be encountered that would make the brutality of Selma seem good-natured by comparison.

The Negro in the North, driven to despair by gradualism and procrastination, could "activate the ghettos" and trigger a variety of violent outbursts against slum housing, inferior schools, unemployment and the hopelessness of urban discrimination.

The Extension of Authority

But wherever the action takes place the Federal Government will find itself in the midst of these local conflicts. The Department of Justice used to be the locus of Federal activity in behalf of civil rights; its responsibility consisted primarily of filing voting discrimination suits under the authority of the Civil Rights Act of 1957, as amended in 1960. But the Civil Rights Act of 1964 extended Federal authority rather dramatically: Title VI, for example, by specifying that Federal funds cannot be used in a discriminatory fashion established the entire Federal bureaucracy as an active participant in the desegregation of schools, colleges, hospitals, agricultural programs and literally hundreds of governmental activities receiving Federal financial assistance.

When Title VII of the act takes effect on July 2, business and labor will confront for the first time a Federal law designed to prevent discrimination in employment and administered by a five-member Equal Employment Opportunity Commission. Although the procedures for enforcing non-discriminatory standards are rather cumbersome and crude, the Federal Government will, nevertheless, be recognized as *the* major source of power in the drive to make non-discrimination in employment more than an empty slogan. Civil rights leaders will surely make the most of this important new ally.

Although the Civil Rights Act of 1964 exempted housing from coverage, it also noted that this exemption did not affect the President's authority to deal with the problem of housing discrimination by executive action. The Johnson Administration is currently scrutinizing most carefully the possibility of expanding President Kennedy's housing order requiring non-discrimination in Veteran's Administration and Federal Housing Authority home mortgages (covering only about 20 percent of the new housing market) to include housing financed by institutions insured by the Federal Deposit Insurance Corporation and the Federal Savings and Loan Insurance Corporation. Thus authority to provide meaningful equal opportunity in housing may be added to the Federal Government's civil rights arsenal.

And Federal involvement extends beyond the limited concept of guaranteeing "civil rights" into the broader realm of promoting "equal opportunity." Such programs as the war on poverty, aid to education, vocational education and manpower training, and expanded health care facilities are valuable tools in combating the root causes of the vicious cycle of discrimination that characterizes life in the Northern ghettos and rural slums.

The emerging situation is clear: in this period of general fragmentation and decentralization of the civil rights movement, the Federal Government finds itself endowed with authority that relates directly to many of the most complex and potentially explosive racial problems North and South.

Transforming Authority into Power

How well prepared is the Government to meet these new responsibilities? Can Federal involvement help continue the record of accomplishment of the past several years and avoid the violence that often occurs when determined men lose faith in their society's ability to remedy long-standing political, economic and social deprivations?

Vice President Hubert Humphrey has the task of answering these two questions. The President has assigned him the staggering job of coordinating and directing the Government's civil rights operations. Humphrey will serve as chairman of the newly established President's Council of Equal Opportunity, an inter-agency committee composed of the executive agencies with major civil rights responsibilities. The Council, assisted by a small staff, will pursue its many assignments through working-level task forces recruited from the operating agencies. Task forces have already been established in the functional areas of employment, education, Federally assisted programs and community relations.

The mind boggles at the administrative knots that must be unraveled. How, for example, do you prevent a situation from arising where the Atomic Energy Commission decides to build a nuclear facility on the same college campus where the Department of Health, Education and Welfare has terminated funds of the National Defense Education loan program due to racial discrimination? What, for example, will be the relationship between the Equal Employment Opportunity Commission—using the cumbersome procedures provided by Title VII of the Civil Rights Act—and the President's Committee on Equal Employment Opportunity—monitoring the Government's contract compliance program under the more efficient and far-reaching standards set forth by Executive Order? How, for example, do you achieve consistency and uniformity of action where such diverse entities as the Department of Justice, the Community Relations Service and the

Office of Economic Opportunity may be enmeshed simultaneously in racial problems within a single locality?

Such purely administrative headaches appear rather tame, and perhaps even irrelevant, in comparison with the turmoil and suffering encountered by persons in the vanguard of the civil rights struggle. Yet the outcome of many local clashes will depend in very large measure upon the effectiveness and impact of the Government's actions in regard to employment, housing, education and voting.

Bureaucratic inertia is the factor that renders impotent many commendable programs initiated by the President or enacted by the Congress. And bureaucratic inertia will be the major enemy in transforming existing Federal civil rights *authority* into effective *power* that is capable of making a difference in the lives of people.

At this writing it is impossible to predict with certainty whether this critical transformation from authority to power will be accomplished. Federal administrators charged for many years with building hospitals (or running the Department of Agriculture's Extension Service, or funding school programs) without regard for the subsequent existence of discrimination in those programs will find it difficult indeed to reorient their operations to comply with Title VI.

Political pressures will be directed frequently toward the Federal establishment by state and local officials anxious to blunt a particular civil rights policy. How, one wonders, would the President respond to a request from a loyal Southern governor to move more slowly in the implementation of Title VI against his state's elementary and secondary schools?

In short, countless factors will be operating to hamper or cripple the execution of the Federal Government's new duties in civil rights. Yet the present disorganized state of affairs within the civil rights groups makes it essential that somehow the sleeping giant of Federal power come to life.

LYNDON JOHNSON AND THE 89TH CONGRESS:
The End of the Beginning?

In these years following the multiple disillusionments of Vietnam, Watergate, Iran-Contra, the Contract with America, Monica Lewinsky, the Florida vote-counting fiasco, the outbreak of corporate lawlessness (Enron, Global Crossing, et al.), the vanishing Weapons of Mass Destruction in Iraq, among other outrages, it is all but impossible to recall that period during the 88th and 89th Congress (1963–1966) when Americans actually admired their national government. Pollster Louis Harris, George Gallup and others routinely recorded percentages of sixty and above of Americans expressing "a great deal of confidence and trust" in the Executive branch, Congress, and the Supreme Court. Not only that, the public consistently looked to the Federal government as the place where the most important questions facing the nation were handled.

As NDP documents in this article, this faith in the efficacy of the national government was well founded. For the first time in a generation, the President and Congress were acting in direct response to a long list of perceived needs—health insurance for older persons, Federal dollars for education at all levels, housing assistance, immigration reform, regional economic development, and on and on. While it is true, as NDP also points out, that many of these initiatives had been accumulating since the Truman years, the tidal surge of enactment swept official Washington off its feet, and pushed popular support of the national government to record high levels.

Under the mantle of the "Great Society," Johnson planned to push well beyond the policies and programs that were cascading into place throughout 1965. As a marker on how far the Federal government has come (or gone, depending on one's perspective), note toward the end of the article NDP's prediction that "the mystical barrier of the $100 billion Federal budget" was soon likely to be breached. Wow. Bush's last proposal to Congress exceeded $2.01 trillion. Yes, we sure do live in dramatically different circumstances.

Johnson's hopes were never fully actualized and his popularity soon began to plunge. NDP speaks of "the commotion among segments of the liberal community over the President's policies in Southeast Asia." In 1965, I never appreciated how this "commotion among segments" would destroy Johnson's political base, erode his popular support, and, in the end, bring his presidency to an ignominious end.

But it did.

"THE END OF THE BEGINNING"?

Lyndon Johnson and the 89th Congress

NICHOLAS D. PICQUE

C&C – September 20, 1965

THE JOHNSON ADMINISTRATION has survived another crisis of the White House budget—and the way in which it did so revealed something about the nature of its legislative record and also high-lighted some interesting Presidential idiosyncrasies.

It seems that President Johnson's string of victories on Capitol Hill, his pitchman's instincts to transform each bill-signing into a state ceremony, and his campaign to promote thriftiness within the White House recently collided in a jumble of Presidential priorities. The pens used by the President to sign new laws were found to cost in excess of $1 each. And his profligate habit of distributing them to everyone within shouting distance—friend and foe alike—had produced an expenditure of over $600 since the 89th Congress convened in January. Could such extravagant behavior by a thrifty President be countenanced? Could Congress continue to pass every Presidential program in sight?

Discreet White House inquiries, however, soon located suitable pens, which wholesaled at just 17 cents each. Everyone breathed easier—Congress could continue passing bills, the President could continue passing out pens and the White House budget could remain inviolate.

While this tale unquestionably adds several solid paragraphs to the growing volumes of Johnsoniana, it also suggests that Congress *has* been passing a large number of important items in the President's program. And it indicates that a broad spectrum of support within both parties has been contributing to these successes.

The commotion among segments of the liberal community over the President's policies in Southeast Asia, coupled with a dislike of his personal style and conduct, has obscured—or rendered irrelevant to many—the Administration's remarkable successes in Congress.

The President not only wins every time out, but his victories are being taken for granted. After fifteen years of repeated failures, passage of the Medicare bill generated hardly any excitement at all—two years ago the Democrats would have danced in the Capitol parking lot. Today a Senator is more apt to smile, shrug and consult the legislative calendar to see what comes next.

At this writing the 89th Congress—hardly pausing from the hectic and productive pace of 1964—has passed such historic laws as voting rights, Medicare, elementary and secondary education, omnibus housing (including the controversial rent supplement plan), the Department of Housing and Urban Development, Appalachia assistance, the Presidential succession amendment and excise tax reductions. Other major proposals with at least a good chance of passing this year include: immigration, repeal of Section 14 (b) of the Taft-Hartley Act, the farm bill, higher education, antipoverty renewal, regional development, and air and water pollution control.

By the end of August Congress had enacted about 50 percent of President Johnson's major legislative requests, with a number of others nearing final passage. By comparison, the first session of the 88th Congress enacted only 27 percent of President Kennedy's program—a figure that included the late spurt of legislative activity following the President's assassination in November.

How He Does It

This excellent record has had a variety of interesting consequences within Congress and throughout Washington generally. There has, for example, been a marked lapse in the drive to reform Congressional rules and procedures. Although a joint Congressional committee is now examining a variety of reform proposals, these efforts are distinguished principally for their lack of urgency. It is, in fact, rather difficult to document the case that Congress is outmoded, sluggish and thwarting the President when one or another major program passes each week.

Meanwhile, the Republican opposition has been almost totally frustrated in its efforts to mount an effective counteroffensive to the Administration's domestic program. While the President rumbles along from victory to victory, House Republican leader Gerald Ford has led his disorganized forces into a series of abortive and damaging encounters.

Ford's shortage of votes is usually so acute that the GOP alternatives—regardless of their merits—are doomed to instant defeat. On occasion the results are even worse, e.g., the Republican effort to sponsor a voting rights bill that would avoid certain constitutional snags found in the Administration's version resulted in an unplanned—and unwanted—alliance with Southern Democrats who viewed the GOP bill as the lesser of two evils.

Not only was the substitute roundly defeated but the President promptly congratulated the House for rejecting "the substitute amendment—supported by the Republican leadership—which would have seriously damaged and diluted the guarantee of the right to vote for all Americans." The feeble Republican reply then gave President Johnson another opportunity to document publicly his conversion to the cause of civil rights.

On those rare occasions when the Administration appears likely to lose on the House floor to a Republican substitute, the President has quickly instructed his Democratic leadership to adopt the opponents' position before the vote can occur. A flurry of last-minute meetings on the omnibus farm bill succeeded in changing the method of financing the wheat certificate plan with the Administration adopting the GOP formula in order to avoid defeat on the "bread tax" issue.

In one instance the President abandoned an issue that appeared likely to produce a major legislative confrontation. When J. Edgar Hoover opposed the consular convention with the Soviet Union, describing it as a "cherished goal of the Soviet intelligence services," President Johnson decided not to rebut the FBI director's testimony and dropped the fight altogether. The convention, which would have permitted a variety of services to U.S. travelers in the Soviet Union— not to mention an opportunity to relax slightly the tensions of the cold war—has been postponed indefinitely.

Sen. Everett Dirksen often speaks about "ideas whose time has come"—those proposals, such as the Civil Rights Act of 1964, that come to the Congress with substantial backing across the country even though they were once controversial. Critics of Johnson tend to dismiss such victories as Medicare and voting rights as examples of these predetermined decisions—only a total incompetent could bungle the job.

This view ignores the ample opportunities that always exist to bungle. Damaging amendments can be adopted on the floor with little warning; vital provisions can be lost in the never-ending bargaining carried on by principal members of both houses; major sections can be lost in conference committee. The potentialities for disaster are limitless. The point, however, is simply this: the errors did not occur, and Medicare and voting rights *did* pass. No other President can make that statement.

In sum, Lyndon Johnson as President has been using with visible success the same general legislative techniques that served him so effectively as majority leader: acquiring blocs of votes in Congress by picking off the leaders of these blocs, adjusting the substance of legislation until a favorable majority is produced, understanding the political milieu of each bill as it relates to key senators and congressmen and acting accordingly, giving close attention to the personal whims and desires of actual or potential opponents (never has a President more frequently invited members of the opposition to the White House for social functions and substantive discussions), and displaying a toughness that demands and receives that extra effort from his supporters.

The success is visible; the record is impressive. Washington is often captivated by the simple act of passing a bill—regardless of the substantive details. But how many members of Congress really understand the details of bills upon which they vote? And how many legislators have time or knowledge to evaluate accurately the impact that their efforts have on the lives of people?

Have We Done Enough?

Admitting that Johnson has been successful in passing his proposals, and admitting that this record compares most favorably with any twentieth century President, one is still required to ask: Are the proposals themselves capable of meeting the complex economic and social problems confronting the nation? How much of the President's success is due to his ability as a national leader and how much depends upon his skill in operating within an existing consensus? What is the nature of the consensus as it relates to improving the lives of Negroes in urban ghettos and poor whites in rural slums?

It is no secret that the President's task forces that reported after the '64 election failed to reveal any truly original propositions for dealing with basic problems afflicting our social and economic order. Johnson's current legislative program consists partially of Kennedy and pre-Kennedy holdovers (e.g., Medicare, immigration, Department of Housing and Urban Development) and partially of original proposals (e.g., elementary and secondary education bill, rent subsidies, regional health centers).

Neither Kennedy nor Johnson, however, can claim to have proposed legislation to deal on a national scale with such fundamental matters as the assimilation of Negro Americans into society and such prior objectives as destruction of the urban ghetto, or the continuing growth of population and related demands for better schools, more livable cities, cleaner environment, etc.

The semi-secret Labor Department study on the disintegration of the Negro family demonstrates clearly that the circumstances of most Negro Americans are worsening, not improving. And measures that have assisted other minority groups in the past are deemed not adequate for this crisis situation. The job of bolstering the resources of Negro Americans, especially in relation to family structure, demands a kind of Federal action never before contemplated—both in terms of the size of Federal expenditure and the depth of involvement in personal and community affairs.

In July the unemployment rate of 4.5 percent was the lowest since October 1957. But July figures also revealed that unemployment among non-white males actually increased—the only category to do so. In the aftermath of the Los Angeles riots, the need for a massive adult work program that would put unemployed Negroes to work—regardless of their training or ability—is clearly evident. It is estimated that about $1 billion annually in such a program would eliminate male unemployment for all practical purposes. But the business community would criticize it as "leaf raking."

In like manner the need for massive amounts of low-income housing is an essential part of any determined effort to destroy the urban ghetto and to revitalize our cities. This will cost a great deal of money and will disrupt the many interests with a heavy financial stake in keeping the urban slums intact. And the appeal among American middle-class citizens—the mainstay of the Johnson consensus—will be limited.

The existing components of the war on poverty fall far short in certain critical areas: poverty among the elderly, rural poverty and the problems of preadolescent youngsters from poverty areas.

Will He Fracture the Consensus?

President Johnson has instructed his advisers to begin preparing programs capable of dealing with these issues—regardless of cost or political liability. But whether or not these proposals ever emerge from the White House is quite another question. The nature of the problems indicates that solutions are not going to come cheaply; they will, moreover, have to produce some manner of income redistribution. It can be safely predicted that large numbers of Americans will find these concepts highly repugnant to their traditional understanding of the division between public and private responsibilities.

Under these circumstances one cannot help ponder this question: Will the tools of Lyndon Johnson's trade—the tools that have served him faithfully as majority leader and President—permit such a quantum jump in the nature of his domestic program? For Lyndon Johnson is a terribly complex man—he sees the need, he feels the need, but he also avoids intuitively the precedent-shattering move that fractures consensus and good feeling. And Lyndon Johnson has to be well-liked.

An unintended consequence of the expanding conflict in South Vietnam will be a need to breach the mystical barrier of the $100 billion Federal budget. When this is done, one can hope the President will listen to his own words (as adapted from Churchill) in the Howard University commencement address—that he will come to understand that his legislative record to date ". . . is not the end; it is not even the beginning of the end; but it is perhaps the end of the beginning."

THE PRESIDENT AND THE CONGRESS:
Congressional Interests Eventually Conflict with the President's

Early in this article, NDP relates a story about an anonymous liberal senator—one known for consistent advocacy of governmental action to resolve public-sector problems—disparaging the Executive branch to a new staff member. Interesting story: the liberal senator was Hubert Humphrey and I was the new staff member. Since I was still working on then Vice President Humphrey's staff in 1966, it seemed appropriate not to attribute the incident to anyone in particular. So, I fudged the details.

In fact, it was April 1961 and I had just arrived in Senator Humphrey's office as a congressional fellow of the American Political Science Association. Humphrey had just won a seat on the prized Appropriations Committee, an assignment he had sought for years. However, in those days of small congressional staffs, no one in Humphrey's office had time to follow appropriations. So I won the honor: a real, concrete legislative assignment with significant responsibility. At age twenty-six, that was exciting business.

Humphrey decided I needed a five-minute orientation. He summoned me into his senatorial office. As I entered, he was signing a huge stack of letters. I waited quietly for the great man to take notice of me. He eventually looked up, recognized me, put down his pen, and spoke:

"John, you are one of those political scientists. I was one of those, too, many years ago. So I know that most political scientists believe it is the President who is in charge in Washington. Congress, for its part, should support the President, especially if the President and Congress are of the same party. The President has a budget and the Congress should support the President . . . a more responsible party system and all that," said Humphrey.

"That's about the way we are taught to see it," I responded.

"Well," said Humphrey, "you are going to be in charge of appropriations around here. I can tell you there are worthy projects and activities not mentioned in the President's budget that need to be pursued through appropriations. BOB [Bureau of the Budget] will always tell you that's impossible and will oppose them, no matter their merit. For example, there should be an agricultural research lab on the St. Paul campus of the University of Minnesota. It needs to be done but it's not in the President's budget and won't be for years. So political scientists will tell us to support the President, and wait. That's the responsible thing to do."

"Well," I said, "I suppose so."

"Now, John, I'm sure you'll do a fine job with appropriations but, from one political scientist to another, I'm going to suggest you follow Humphrey's Rule. Do that, and you will be a great success."

I waited for what seemed to be a very long time, but finally had to ask: "What, Senator, is Humphrey's Rule?"

"It's a simple rule," he said. "It expresses one of the eternal truths of American democracy. Remember it always . . . and it is: *The Executive branch is always wrong!* Can you remember that?"

I allowed that I could handle that. And so I did in the coming weeks, scheming with constituents and renegade bureaucrats to advance various projects through the Appropriations subcommittees on which Humphrey served. BOB (now the Office of Management and Budget) be damned. As a matter of fact, one of the earliest triumphs was the ag research lab on the St. Paul campus.

Thus, I received a valuable lesson in Madisonian democracy. But Humphrey's light-hearted banter with a green-as-grass congressional fellow had another and far more contentious dimension. NDP observes: "Congress and the President scrapping—situation normal." But normality was not what Lyndon Johnson had in mind or was used to. As the many meritorious biographies of Johnson have made clear, LBJ simply hated to lose, couldn't stand it, and would go to most any length to avoid it. His entire *modus operandi,* developed through years of effort, was designed to ensure victory through one tactic or another: flattery, threats, information, arm-twisting, blandishments, bribes, trickery, rational argument, patriotic appeals, personal attacks, or whatever.

The Johnson Treatment, however applied, worked for him as majority leader and for the first two years of his presidency— 1964–1965. Now, by 1966, the constitutional designs of James Madison and the growing disaffection with the Vietnam conflict rendered the Johnson Treatment almost inoperable. What was LBJ to do in circumstances that he had rarely encountered in his long and successful political career?

By all accounts, Johnson was more contentious and disagreeable than usual during these bitter times. How did his browbeaten staff, how did Lady Bird, how did his Vice President, stand it? From the vantage point of the VP's offices in the Executive Office Building, across West Executive Drive from the West Wing, it wasn't pretty.

The Founding Fathers knew what they were talking about, even when it came to Lyndon Johnson.

"CONGRESSIONAL INTERESTS EVENTUALLY CONFLICT WITH THE PRESIDENT'S"

The President and the Congress

NICHOLAS D. PICQUE

C&C – March 21, 1966

WHAT ACCOUNTS for the frayed tempers and thinly veiled insults encountered on Capitol Hill and in the White House these days? Has the issue of Vietnam dissipated the heady feeling of confidence and accomplishment that distinguished the last session of Congress? Or has Lyndon Johnson lost his touch?

The Washington press corps, following a vigorous round of cannibalizing each other's stories, has produced the following verdict: President Johnson has become surprisingly indifferent to the opinions of his former colleagues, and a little disdainful as well. The vaunted consensus is about to disappear. The future is murky and unpredictable. Congress is in revolt against its former master.

But James Madison had another answer. Writing in *The Federalist* about the "partition of powers" among the three branches of government, he observed, "Ambition must be made to counteract ambition." And there is one characteristic of Madison's system of separated and ambitious powers that should be noted: *it works*. American history teaches again and again: Congressional interests eventually conflict with the interests of the President. The common bond of political party is not sufficient to keep members of Congress and the President from regarding each other with varying degrees of distrust, contempt and antagonism.

It is sometimes difficult to appreciate the depth of the feeling of institutional identity and independence that permeates the Congress vis-a-vis the Executive Branch. One prominent Senator—a liberal who staunchly advocated increased governmental action in many areas—expressed this attitude precisely when he announced this rule of thumb to a new staff member: "Remember this about the Executive Branch, they are always wrong."

Congress acquiesces when the President determines its agenda each session through submission of his legislative program, but it stoutly reserves the right to alter this legislation as necessary or to ignore certain bills altogether. There are, moreover, definite limits to the President's ability to combat guerrilla warfare once it breaks out on Capitol Hill; members of Congress who specialize in proclaiming their independence from their Chief seldom discover this to be a political liability back home. In this difficult environment Lyndon Johnson's most surprising legislative achievement has been the era of relatively good feeling that lasted for two sessions.

It is evident this era is ending. For some persons this is startling news. But for those of Madisonian perspective, another conclusion is likely: "Congress and the President scrapping—situation normal."

The Spirit of Rebellion Rises

Congressional discomfort appears to be related primarily to America's growing involvement in Vietnam. Without question this unhappy and complex matter is a contributing factor. But it is important not to overlook several acts of Congressional defiance unrelated to Vietnam that occurred at the end of last session: the defeat of home rule for the District of Columbia, the failure to repeal Section 14 (b) of the Taft-Hartley Act, and the elimination of funds for the rent supplement program and the National Teacher Corps.

Was it portent or just coincidence that President Johnson's orchestrated extravaganza, "A Salute to Congress," was presented to a half-empty auditorium—the entire membership of the House missing the tribute to battle over the First Lady's highway beautification bill? Members of Congress had repeatedly gone the limit for the President and his extensive legislative program. Dozens of historic measures had become law. And as both houses lurched toward adjournment early in October, the spirit of rebellion was in the air.

To understand the reasons for this late-season disenchantment with the Great Society, it is helpful to examine several factors that contributed to Mr. Johnson's remarkable success earlier in the year. The crushing defeat of Barry Goldwater produced not only momentum to sustain a comprehensive legislative program but also helped elect seventy-one freshman Democrats for a net increase of thirty-eight Democratic seats in the House.

In seven of the seventeen key House votes, including such issues as foreign aid, change of House rules, the anti-poverty bill and the Department of Housing and Urban Development, these additional Democrats provided the margin of victory for Mr. Johnson. In most other major bills he relied heavily upon the large contingent of freshman Democrats; and he received their votes 80 percent of the time.

Is this level of support likely to continue? As the November elections draw closer, these freshmen will become increasingly independent in their voting. Running for re-election without the aid of Presidential coattails and the specter of Barry Goldwater's twitching finger on the nuclear button, these men will be tempted to reflect more accurately the opinions of their respective districts, opinions generally more conservative than their voting records to date. Self-preservation—not party loyalty—will become more prevalent as November approaches.

Another factor should be noted. Many of the President's victories of the first session, e.g., Medicare, elementary and secondary education, immigration, the Department of Housing and Urban Development, had been debated in one form or another for many years. Their passage, following the November landslide, was almost assured. To this extent Mr. Johnson was cashing in chips that had already been won, a situation not likely to produce serious opposition or disquiet among members of his party. But last year's victories depleted the larder. And as this stock is replenished with new proposals, the potential for opposition will rise accordingly.

Although the Constitution encourages active competition between the two branches, it usually takes a specific issue to initiate an actual confrontation. Vietnam is surely such an issue. Without becoming embroiled in the merits of current policy, it is clear the Chief Executive's responsibility for the conduct of the war far outstrips that of any individual Senator or Representative. The burden of ultimate decision rests with the President, who is denied the luxury of a second guess or a second chance. And so *he* decides. Congress is free to criticize and chastise whichever direction he moves—although, in the end, as we have just seen, it will provide the funds and other support requested by the President.

The Republican activists can be expected to exploit the Vietnam crisis in at least two directions. First, they will stoutly support a broadened U.S. involvement, especially bombing of North Vietnam, while simultaneously noting how peculiar it is that every time a Democrat is President we find ourselves at war. Second, the issue will be used as the entering wedge to cut into funds needed to implement domestic programs of education, civil rights, the war on poverty, health, farm support and foreign aid.

In the Dark Recesses

For this reason, many of the critical legislative battles of this session will occur in the dark recesses of Appropriations subcommittees. Here people rarely look; what is even more unfortunate is that they understand so little of what they may occasionally see. Public commotion and support abound for many vital programs on their initial passage, but when it comes time to appropriate the money, the crowds and supporters have gone home and the programs come under the intense scrutiny of the men who opposed them in the first place. Entire programs can be emasculated in minutes by denying funds for operating and administrative expenses, and months may elapse before this is evident to the public.

For example, effective enforcement of the Federal Government's civil rights programs now depends largely upon the number of people available to carry out routine administrative functions: inspection of school and hospital desegregation, evaluation of desegregation plans, filing of lawsuits, mediation between the Federal Government and local officials, etc. This year for the first time the Federal budget contains enough money to support detailed and rigorous administrative action to secure compliance with existing law. But this budget item must survive an expected two-pronged assault from Southern Democrats and conservative Republicans if the expanded program is actually to become a reality. Similar challenges await most of the Great Society programs inaugurated last year.

The war on poverty is the other specific issue capable of fostering a serious confrontation between Congress and Lyndon Johnson this session. The combination of sloppy administration, poor public relations, well-publicized failures and little-known successes, fights with mayors and other local officials, and criticism from both the extreme Left and Right has made deep inroads in the strong support initially accorded the war on poverty. Almost every Senator and Congressman has had some incredible encounter with the poverty warriors of the Office of Economic Opportunity, and enthusiastic supporters in Congress are almost non-existent.

What, then, awaits President Johnson on Capitol Hill this session and in the future? It seems most doubtful that last year's record will be duplicated again soon.

It is not surprising that the capital is alive with stories of revolts and rebellions, but Washington has a short memory. Long since forgotten are Kennedy's troubles in 1962 and 1963, Eisenhower's and Truman's disappointments, Roosevelt's defeats, and so on back to Washington's rebuff by the Senate when he sought its advice and consent on an Indian treaty. Johnson's achievements last session perhaps outrank any single session of Congress. This level of performance seems too atypical to serve as a basis for judging this or future Congresses.

Washington also forgets the remarkable political and legislative skills of Lyndon Johnson. He is human, to be sure, but he still ranks as one of the most effective legislative leaders in American history.

"Congress and the President scrapping—situation normal," sums up the current state of affairs accurately. Under these conditions Mr. Johnson is probably capable of achieving his more important legislative objectives—if not the grand slam engineered last year.

CONGRESS AND THE URBAN CRISIS:
Have the People Grown Weary?

How do public attitudes and beliefs translate into legislative action? That's the perennial question of representative democracy that NDP examines in this article.

The American people were sick of civil rights activism, urban disruptions, and far-ranging schemes of the Great Society. Vietnam was an issue growing in intensity, spreading disillusionment and discord across the land. As a consequence, Congress in 1968 was unwilling to move ahead with domestic proposals directed at the ills of urban America and ignored or defeated most of what Lyndon Johnson tried to do. That was the conventional reality, as determined and propagated by Washington news outlets and congressional spokespersons.

Where did this conventional reality come from? As NDP points out, there existed ample survey research findings to conclude the public still was willing to move forward with an expanded Federal assault on urban ills. But the movers and shakers in Congress simply ignored this intelligence. That's not what "the people" wanted, so Congress muttered disagreeable sentiments and did next to nothing.

Those puzzling circumstances in 1968 are remarkably similar to what prevailed two years ago in Nashville where the Tennessee General Assembly struggled unsuccessfully to reform the state's dysfunctional and unjust tax system. The conventional reality was indisputable: everybody knew that Tennesseans despised the income tax. Regardless of what other ghastly fates befell the state, the income tax must not prevail. That was the political reality dominating the General Assembly all session long.

But a closer look at public attitudes in Tennessee suggested quite another reality, not unlike what the Harris Survey found to be true in 1968. In a series of credible polls, a solid majority of Tennesseans— ranging from 52 percent to more than 60 percent—in fact favored a package of tax changes that linked a cut in the state sales tax, elimination of the tax on food, non-prescription drugs, and clothing, and elimination of the tax on interest and dividends with a low flat-rate or graduated income tax. But this reality did not accord with what everyone "knew" to be true. So these findings were simply ignored.

Not in dispute by anyone in Tennessee were the enormous majorities—exceeding 80 percent—in opposition to a further sales tax increase to close the $1 billion shortfall in the state budget. Yet, the ideological fervor by a minority of Tennesseans opposed to the income tax, even when combined with lower sales taxes and elimination of the food tax, was sufficiently robust to overwhelm the tax reform package, kill the income tax, and adopt a full one percent increase in the sales tax, giving Tennessee the highest sales tax rate in the country. Representative democracy in Tennessee had gone haywire—such is the power of whatever the conventional reality happens to be at a moment in time.

The reality of belief in 2002 was just as hard to understand as what NDP was reporting in 1968. Who decides what is reality? How does it take root and flourish? How is it possible for this reality to overwhelm contrary views grounded in actual public attitudes?

The article suggests several ways to approach this enigma and need not be repeated here. But another piece of the puzzle subsequently was suggested in my book, *One Last Chance: The Democratic Party, 1974–1976* (Praeger, 1974). In 1964, two political scientists—Lloyd Free and Hadley Cantril—discovered a peculiar form of political schizophrenia: persons tended toward conservatism when issues were cast in ideological terms (strong support for the proposition that "the Federal government is interfering too much in state and local matters").

However, when the issue was focused on specific operational matters, the same respondents tended toward a more "liberal" activist approach (equal, or even stronger, support for the statement that "the Federal government has a responsibility to work with states and localities to improve education"). This ideological/operational split in public attitudes was further tested in polling conducted by the Gallup Organization for my book. The findings were a robust reaffirmation of the Free and Cantril thesis of 1964.

The same phenomenon helps explain the strong ideological opposition to an income tax. ("The state government has no right to penalize your economic success through an income tax."), and the solid support recorded for the comprehensive reform package of elimination or cuts in the sales tax and enactment of a compensatory income tax ("Would you support a tax package that contained sales tax reductions or their total elimination along with a low graduated tax on incomes?").

If this analysis has a ring of truth, it also suggests that legislative bodies deal far more readily, more easily, with ideological reality than with more complex operational proposals, for whatever complicated reasons. Breaking through this ideological barrier was no easier in Washington during the final year of Johnson's presidency than it was in Tennessee some thirty-four years later.

HAVE THE PEOPLE GROWN WEARY?

Congress and the Urban Crisis

NICHOLAS D. PICQUE

C&C – March 4, 1968

A STRIKING characteristic of the 90th Congress has been the inability of persons advocating a massive response to the urban crisis—both inside and outside Congress—to make more headway.

This is conventionally explained as follows: most members of Congress believe their actions on major issues are a true reflection of public opinion. By some mystical process of political osmosis, the real wants and needs of the people are made known to their elected Representatives in Washington. Accordingly, the slashing of President Johnson's appropriation requests for Model Cities, rent supplements and the poverty program, the initial defeat of the rat control bill and the passage of the anti-riot bill in the House are symptomatic of a growing national disgust with Negroes, the civil rights movement, riots and those Federal programs designed to relieve hard-pressed city administrations. Congress balks when the people grow weary.

Four years ago the public enthusiastically supported the civil rights legislation designed to establish legal equality in such areas as voting, employment and public accommodations. Congress, so the argument runs, sensed this wave of public opinion and passed the Civil Rights Act of 1964 and the Voting Rights Act of 1965. Today, the same drive for economic, social and political equality founders as the majority of white Americans turn their backs on the Negro revolution.

Conflicting Evidence on the Nation's Attitude

This analysis, its wide acceptance notwithstanding, overlooks much conflicting evidence. Last November, for example, pollster Louis Harris reported that "three months after major rioting swept over fifty American cities, a majority of the American people still favors a massive Governmental program to root out the causes of ghetto discontent." The Harris Survey found that 57 percent of the people favored a Federal program to tear down ghettos in the cities with 32 percent opposed. Harris concluded his November analysis with this observation: " . . . the American people have a deep sense of urgency about the government undertaking an unprecedented program to wipe out what people have become convinced are major causes of violence and unrest." Have the people, in fact, grown weary?

From the battle which raged on the House floor last session over the poverty program amendments, one might have concluded that a massive campaign to destroy the program was underway across America. If such a campaign existed, it ranks as one of the more low-key lobbying efforts in Congressional history. Out of the 100 witnesses to appear before the House Committee on Education and Labor, only *one* proposed that the poverty program be abolished. The legislation passed in the Senate by the largest margin since its inception even though the bill submitted by the Administration had been considerably strengthened. Yet the battle on the House floor was bitterly fought and only narrowly won.

Again, given the total lack of progress in the Senate to enact a national non-discrimination in housing law, one might have supposed that local efforts to ban housing discrimination would suffer a similar fate. In fact, the number of local fair housing ordinances *doubled* in 1967 so that today more than half the U.S. population lives in cities or states with such provisions. Forty-seven local fair housing laws had been passed since New York City enacted the nation's first in 1958. In 1967, forty-seven more were approved. Have the people grown weary?

Finally, the capacity of Congress to sense the mood of the American people on these social and economic issues was directly raised in another Harris Survey. In January, Harris reported that 59 percent of his national sample gave the 90th Congress a negative job rating. "Specific criticisms of last year's session," Harris noted, "are directed at failure to pass a gun control bill, cutting back aid to cities, not passing an open-housing law and cutting funds for the poverty program."

Such general survey data fails, of course, to take into account the disproportionate influence wielded by committee chairmen and other key Congressmen and Senators. Particularly in the House, a powerful chairman such as Wilbur Mills of the Committee on Ways and Means can distort to some degree the choices that confront the general membership of the House. On the other hand, no human being is all-powerful, not even Wilbur Mills, and seldom can a committee chairman indefinitely prevent the House from acting on issues that command the firm backing of a significant majority of the members.

It is, in short, too easy an explanation simply to blame committee chairmen or other aspects of the legislative system when Congress fails to act in a desired manner. One must always look further to determine just how the general membership felt on the issue and how much leverage the members were willing to exert to achieve the desired objective.

There is, then, evidence that suggests that Congress is considerably out of touch with a majority of the American people and that significant support exists for expanded Governmental initiatives in attacking the interlocking problems of the urban ghetto. If this is accurate, a crucial opportunity is being squandered by persons who are failing to translate this general public attitude into specific programs of action.

Shattering Congressional Illusions

Although Congressmen may honestly believe they are reflecting constituent demands when they vote to emasculate the Model Cities program, these same legislators could operate with considerably wider latitude on the issue if the advocates of the program functioned more effectively. Most voters fail even to recognize their Representative's name, much less are they interested in the specifics of his voting record.

A Congressman's view of his district, moreover, often constitutes a type of self-fulfilling prophecy. He generally hears from people with whom he agrees and tends to interpret what he hears in ways that support his preconceived notions. On a given issue, in short, the image of his district's feeling is often based on highly unrepresentative fragments and assumptions.

When a large segment of the Congress opposes legislation aimed at the urban crisis, as it surely did during the first session of the 90th Congress, the task becomes one of shattering these Congressional illusions and misconceptions of what the American people really want. This calls for a skillfully designed and shrewdly executed campaign to dramatize the issues and mobilize the broad support that apparently exists. The almost miraculous explosion of pro-consumer sentiment in the 90th Congress (illustrated by the overwhelming triumph of the Truth-in-Lending legislation in the House) is only the most recent example of how a lost cause can be turned into a major victory.

In 1964–65, for example, the churches zeroed in on doubtful Republican Senators from the Midwest and turned them around on the pending civil rights legislation. But in 1967–68, persons working actively to capitalize on the latent support for urban and civil rights legislation could be jammed into one elevator in the Rayburn House Office Building. Let no one underestimate the cost of this failure to organize and to act.

The seemingly endless struggle in Vietnam is obviously a major reason for this abdication on the domestic front. The multitudes of anti-war activists may be correct in asserting that nothing else matters until this tragic encounter is ended. But those who demonstrate such moral conviction in opposing Lyndon Johnson on Vietnam to the exclusion of fighting *for* a massive assault on the urban ghettos must also recognize one direct effect of this withdrawal: the 90th Congress will continue its work in a state of seeming unconcern over the crisis in our cities.

Is the President too Preoccupied?

But what about Lyndon Johnson himself? Surely he, as President, has the sworn duty to escalate the War on Poverty and related programs. It is, moreover, precisely because of his fixation on Vietnam that America is denied the leadership and resources that are so desperately needed on the domestic front.

There is no doubt that until the conflict in Vietnam ends, a price will be extracted in terms of Presidential leadership and Federal expenditures on domestic programs. But let no one overlook another equally valid fact of political life: Presidents not only lead; they also follow. John F. Kennedy sent the omnibus Civil Rights Act of 1964 to Congress after the dramatic confrontation in Birmingham in May 1963. In February the President had sent a rather timid civil rights message to Congress, one that little resembled the sweeping package of precedent-shattering proposals that quickly emerged after the police dogs and firehoses were turned on Martin Luther King, Jr. and his followers. The upsurge of organized public sentiment made the difference.

The Administration's domestic program outlined in the State of the Union Message reflects the tight priorities imposed by the dual pressures of defense spending and an economy-minded Congress. Through considerable reshuffling of funds, President Johnson has asked for a $2.1 billion manpower program with major emphasis on hiring the hardcore unemployed, a one billion dollar Model Cities program and a $2.2 billion appropriation for the poverty program. Other increases have been proposed for child health, air pollution, law enforcement and housing. Even though the total increase in these domestic areas has been held to about $500 million by reductions in other parts of the budget, the parsimonious attitude of Congress last session and their continued refusal to pass the President's tax increase make it most unlikely that even these requests will be realized.

The urban crisis surely demands expenditures far in excess of these levels. Just the immediate objective of providing comprehensive job and education programs in the summer for ghetto youngsters would require another $400–$500 million. A longer range goal of building 10 million new dwelling units for ghetto residents would call for about $200 billion.

One can advance the hypothesis that Lyndon Johnson would more likely consider programs of this dimension if Congress had refrained from imposing a reduction of $4 billion in domestic spending last session or if his tax bill was not held hostage as the means of cutting off additional requests for domestic programs. What are the advocates of higher spending prepared to do about these legislative realities?

There is, moreover, the further consideration of what is likely to happen once defense spending drops to a more normal peacetime level. Those who believe that Congress will obligingly transfer the money being spent in Vietnam into domestic programs need only examine what happened when the Korean War ended. The Eisenhower Administration and the Congress launched no massive attack on our domestic ills but instead reduced taxes.

Dramatizing the Message

If Louis Harris is correct, the American people *are* ready for a vastly accelerated attack on the root causes of rioting and despair in our urban ghettos. The problem is now one of dramatizing that message in terms that the 90th Congress can understand.

A potential source of this dramatization could be the report of the National Commission on Civil Disorders now scheduled for release about March 1. The Commission reportedly has documented in the most vivid and explicit language the choice now facing the United States: eliminate the sources of riots or be prepared for a downward spiral of violence and repression ending in the virtual splitting of society, blacks separated from whites, and the urban ghettos isolated from the rest of America. The response of both Congress and the Executive Branch to his analysis will be indeed critical.

It is in this context also that Martin Luther King's projected Poor People's Campaign for Jobs or Income becomes truly significant. Scheduled to begin April 1 in Washington, this effort at militant non-violence and direct action is likely to be the major organized effort to reach the Congress on these crucial issues. Already condemned by many militant Negro activists as old-fashioned and irrelevant while simultaneously being criticized by members of Congress as threatening coercion and intimidation, King's campaign could reveal whether the forces supposedly in favor of expanded Governmental action are able to drive their message home.

Although they may not realize it now, the well-established members of the Urban Coalition, the group organized in the aftermath of the Newark and Detroit riots to lobby for the cities, are likely to be faced with a moment of truth when Dr. King comes to town. If they are unable to devise ways to assist the Poor People's Campaign, and if other natural allies, such as the churches, are equally ineffective, the likelihood of King's failure to affect the 90th Congress, as well as his personal humiliation, would appear great.

And this failure, in turn, would increase dramatically the likelihood of bloodshed, disorder and sharp repression that can only make more distant any massive assault on poverty and the ghettos.

CAUTION AND CONTROL IN THE WHITE HOUSE:
Crises and Controversy Come with the Presidency

In this concluding article, I am able to send NDP into retirement, a condition from which he has not emerged for the last thirty-five years. By January 1969, the Johnson-Humphrey administration had packed its bags and my concerns for anonymity had evaporated. Rest in peace, Nicholas D. Picque. Welcome back, J. G. Stewart.

My core thesis for this piece was to wonder aloud whether Richard Nixon had the guts to be President. I talk about whether he had a willingness to act in circumstances not fully in his control, whether he would run risks to meet challenges and live with controversy, and whether he would speak forthrightly about the unavoidable hard choices facing America. Could the nation come to trust him? As proved to be true with my article on the Goldwater candidacy in 1964, many of the questions I posed then have a surprising contemporary relevance to the presidency of George W. Bush.

However, never in my wildest imaginings did I (or anyone else, for that matter) anticipate what control, controversy, risks, forthrightness, and trust would come to mean in the Nixon years. How could we anticipate his determination to control events by whatever means necessary, even breaking and entering? Or running the most extraordinary risks by planning in the Oval Office to subvert our constitutional system? Or abandoning any pretense of forthrightness in attempting to cover up this plot? Or in demonstrating near total indifference to the system of values that a democracy needs to survive?

How could any reasonably sane Washington observer in January 1969 anticipate such behavior?

But, by the same token, who could have predicted that Richard Nixon, poster boy of the old China Lobby, would travel to mainland China and recognize the Communist regime as its legitimate government? Or that he would travel to Moscow and sign the SALT agreement controlling offensive nuclear weapons? Or that he would, in the early 1970s, approve the basic structure of environmental protections that endures to this day?

And, lest we forget, it was also Nixon who invaded Cambodia, expanded the bombing of North Vietnam, and on whose watch some 25,000 American troops lost their lives, nearly half of all Vietnam-related deaths.

Most of these years I spent at the Democratic National Committee, doing my best to fuel the rhetorical assaults on the various real or perceived outrages of the Nixon crowd. Due to this assignment, I happened to receive a fateful phone call in the early hours of June 17, 1972, to the effect that unidentified burglars had been apprehended in the DNC offices at the Watergate. Did I want to come down to the D.C. police precinct house to sign a complaint? No, I really didn't want to do that at 2:45A.M. and I managed to con the DNC's deputy chairman into performing that historic act. Once again, I successfully dodged the pages of history.

Had Nancy and I a crystal ball at 2:45A.M., June 17, 1972, and had we discerned the future from that moment in time, including Nixon's lurching departure onto the Marine helicopter following his resignation from office, we surely would have dropped in our tracks.

No, none of these things ran through my mind in January 1969. I asked questions that I thought were relevant and on target. How could I, or anyone, have known they were as out of touch with Nixon's future reality as anyone could have imagined?

CRISES AND CONTROVERSY COME WITH THE PRESIDENCY
Caution and Control
C&C – January 20, 1969

PERHAPS WE are just wiser about the likelihood of anyone coming up with quick or easy answers to our complicated and frustrating problems at home and overseas. Perhaps we are still recovering our senses and perspective from the multiple shocks of the past year. Or perhaps the genuine Republicans haven't yet arrived in Washington, D.C.

But whatever the reasons, the mood of the nation's capital as the Nixon Administration moves in could not be more different from the heady, optimistic climate that infected this city when the Presidency last changed hands eight years ago. One need not dwell on the triumphs and failures of the Kennedy-Johnson years to make the point that in 1961 people believed that John F. Kennedy and his bright young men *could* make a difference, that they were willing to run risks in the cause of a more humane and just world, and that things could be set right again.

This blend of self-confidence and eager expectancy dominated John Kennedy's Inaugural Address. Personal sacrifice in the cause of democratic government all at once made sense. Opportunities to serve were eagerly sought by the energetic men who came to occupy the White House and the Executive agencies.

Today the incoming Administration has adopted a posture of somber caution, one ill-suited to spark the imagination of anyone but the most committed Nixonite.

We are told not to expect any far-reaching legislative program from the new Administration. The President will not attempt to mount a

100-day crash effort on Capitol Hill. Energies will be directed primarily to staffing the Federal agencies with "competent" and "young"
executives and to straightening out the bureaucratic morass left by
free-wheeling Democratic programming.

President Nixon will proceed carefully, step-by-step, in evolving a
grand design that will permit rational decision-making, rather than
the case-by-case reacting to events with which Nixon repeatedly
charged the Johnson-Humphrey Administration in the campaign. This
approach will supposedly build a capacity to control, rather than be
controlled by events at home and abroad.

So the changing of the Presidential guard has gone forward with a
minimum of friction, as well as a minimum of excitement. Indeed, the
only surprise in the President-elect's announcement of his Cabinet
occurred when he managed to introduce the Secretary of Commerce
without mentioning his name.

This is, of course, not all bad. Overselling and the indiscriminate raising of expectations were serious shortcomings of both Kennedy and
Johnson. The personal magnetism of John Kennedy and his associates
had only marginal effect on a doubting, and at times recalcitrant,
Congress. None of our current problems— urban decay, race, inflation,
Vietnam, nuclear arms control, among others—will become solvable
simply because a President projects well on television.

The Erosion of Trust

But neither does our democracy function successfully unless the
people—however defined—trust their national leaders and unless they
are able to raise the people's sights about what are legitimate and
desirable goals of national policy.

Trust is eroded by more than a President playing games with the
White House press corps, although Lyndon Johnson's propensity in this
regard surely helped produce his credibility problem. Trust disappears
when a significant portion of the population comes to believe, rightly or

wrongly, that their interests are not being considered by the President; when the President conspicuously fails to deal forthrightly with the urgent business at hand; or when he fails to challenge and inspire.

Given the character of Richard Nixon's campaign for the Presidency, his continuing emphasis on deliberation and caution—his ardent desire to control events—raises a valid question of motive: Does the Nixon style arise from an honest appreciation of the terribly complex problems he will confront as President, or does it arise from a more basic failure of nerve to risk the hard and controversial decisions that are essential to progress? Does it reflect a belief that artful manipulation can substitute for the more potentially controversial course of telling the American people what must be done if we are to prevail in these troubled times?

Throughout the campaign, whether on television or in person, Nixon appeared in a carefully controlled and hand-tailored environment designed to eliminate surprises and the risk of controversy. To claim that this campaign strategy succeeded ignores the far more significant fact that no Presidential candidate ever frittered away so large a lead in so short a time. In terms of making up ground in the national polls, Hubert Humphrey in October surpassed even Harry Truman's remarkable performance in the 1948 race.

The story of the 1968 campaign, indeed, is not that Richard Nixon won but that he almost blew a lead of 15 percentage points. What, then, can one expect in the pressure cooker of the American Presidency? If there is one thing a President finds it difficult to do, it is to execute the responsibilities of his office in an environment free of risk, uncertainty and controversy. The world turns, crises come uninvited and human beings often behave in perverse and irrational ways.

There is, in sum, a basic contradiction between Nixon's apparent concern over controlling events with a minimum of controversy and the conflicting pressures and demands inherent to the Presidency, especially at this point in history. Nixon's actions in resolving this conflict will largely determine the character and record of his administration. And the pattern should be clear before the cherry blossoms bloom on the Potomac.

The problems of racial unrest and the nuclear arms race are illustrative. Some optimists have expressed the hope that the racial violence and destruction of recent years may now be receding, that we may be entering a period of relative tranquility where the racial struggle will be carried forward in a less violent manner. But recent events such as the New York City school dispute, the confrontations at San Francisco State College and the flight of Eldridge Cleaver to avoid arrest cast considerable doubt on this assessment.

How does the new President propose to handle the racial crisis? No one knows, although two things are certain: one, his proposals about black capitalism are sufficient only to a small dimension of the total racial situation, and two, the necessity for decisive Presidential action will not evaporate simply because this fails to accord with Nixon's preference for moving cautiously in circumstances of his own choosing.

More to the point is the fact that certain major features of Nixon's campaign would, if implemented as he proposed, seriously exacerbate racial tensions in America. His proposals about stopping crime in the streets, inflation, and reordering the delivery systems for dispensing Federal aid through revenue sharing, tax incentives, and bloc grants all have the potential for causing serious "blacklash."

The problem of inflation is serious. But if a significant rise in unemployment becomes the Administration's principal weapon for cooling off the economy, and if the bulk of this unemployment occurs in urban slum neighborhoods, the result could be a national crisis far more severe than the present inflation. Similarly, if the Nixon anticrime drive assumes a focus that is primarily antiblack, we could find ourselves caught in a downward spiral of black violence and police repression. Sustained guerilla activity in our major cities is not as far-fetched as some would believe.

Most people familiar with existing procedures for channeling Federal aid to cities, schools, housing, manpower projects and the like agree with the need to develop improved delivery systems. Lack of coordination among Federal agencies, the proliferation of programs in certain functional areas, and the burden that Federal bureaucratic decision-making places on local officials are well-known and recognized problems. But the feasible alternatives to these procedures, particularly in the shortrun, are much less defined.

For one thing, present beneficiaries of these programs are not likely to accept passively any scheme, such as revenue sharing, tax incentives or bloc grants, which threatens their continued participation simply because some bureaucratic red tape will be eliminated in the process. Nor will they sit quietly on the sidelines if the Nixon Administration appears to be reducing or eliminating existing programs as a means of providing funds for bloc grants, the sharing of Federal tax revenues, or tax incentives to benefit private corporations. These experiments would seemingly have to await the availability of new Federal money stemming from increased Federal tax receipts. And the amount of this money would, in turn, be directly related to Nixon's decisions on national security.

These decisions on the operation of Federal programs come to sharp focus in the debate over the nature of community participation and control. Both sides of this controversy have been guilty of excessive sloganeering and empty rhetoric on more than one occasion. The ridiculously low level of community participation in elections to select members for Model Cities projects, for example, suggests that only a small, although vocal, minority of ghetto residents is ready to assume the burden of planning and implementing this complex Federal program. To what degree does this situation really produce an honest expression of community opinion?

At the same time, it is simply no longer debatable that *some* meaningful role for local residents must be devised. The nature of this role will probably vary from city to city and it may be quite different from anything attempted so far. But unless Nixon and associates are willing to experiment and search out viable forms of community involvement—and thereby risk some opposition from the comfortable Americans who elected him—the President's professed objective of healing the divisions among us is almost certain to be dashed in violent and bitter controversy.

One other area should be examined from this perspective. Who will Nixon appoint to such critical positions as the Justice Department's civil rights division, the Labor Department's office of Federal contract compliance, and the office of the civil rights in the Department of Health, Education and Welfare? Who will be nominated as U.S. Attorneys in the Southern states? Who will Nixon send to the Supreme Court?

If the President's strategy of caution and the avoidance of risk means listening only to Senator Strom Thurmond and like persons, the reverberations throughout the civil rights community will be swift and far-reaching. A decision to initiate a period of token Federal compliance with the civil rights statutes and court decisions of the past decade not only would generate anger and hostility from men who have steadfastly rejected the demagoguery of black radicalism, but it would also cripple Nixon's future efforts to achieve some personal credibility on the racial issue.

Living with Controversy

How the President decides to balance and sift these conflicting demands on the racial front will tell us a great deal about his longer-term conduct of the Presidency. But to believe that he can proceed successfully without controversy would be to misunderstand profoundly the dynamics of our contemporary racial situation.

On the question of the nuclear arms race, Nixon will have to decide whether to take seriously his campaign allegations about a security gap and whether he really intends to achieve decisive military superiority over the Soviet Union, rather than settling for a condition of parity. If he goes along with the military chiefs in building a new generation of exotic and expensive weapons, two results are certain: he will mortgage all realistic hope of obtaining significant amounts of additional Federal money for domestic use (thereby also relinquishing the opportunity of developing new delivery systems for Federal aid) and he will place major obstacles in the path of initiating serious negotiations with the Soviet Union over the control of offensive and defensive weapons systems. Nixon's credentials will be further tested by his decision on ratification of the nuclear non-proliferation treaty. A continuation of his campaign position ("I support the treaty but not now . . .") would put beyond reach any realistic hope of cooling off the nuclear arms race in the foreseeable future.

As in the instance of Nixon's dilemma over the racial crisis, the initial decisions relating to arms control will demand from the new President the qualities of enlightened leadership and courage rarely exhibited in the campaign or in Nixon's prior public career. Progress in both areas will require a willingness to act in circumstances not fully under the President's control, to run risks, to live with controversy, and to speak forthrightly about the hard choices this nation cannot avoid in the immediate future.

This is what being President of the United States is all about. And there is little evidence in the post-election period to suggest that President Nixon gets the message.

EXCERPTS FROM
"A TRIBUTE TO REINHOLD NIEBUHR"
by Vice President Hubert H. Humphrey upon the 25th anniversary celebration of Christianity and Crisis

U.S. involvement in Vietnam undoubtedly cost Hubert Humphrey the Presidency. His natural constituency of liberal supporters and groups working for arms control and world peace found his loyal support of Lyndon Johnson's policy of escalation deeply troubling. And Humphrey's incapacity as Vice President to follow his natural instincts on the issue slowly undermined his own self-confidence. When it came time to fight for his own version of the Vietnam platform plank at the 1968 Democratic National Convention, he backed away in the face of LBJ's vitriolic opposition. Chaos at the convention ensued. It was only after he finally spoke his mind on a nationally televised address in late September that his stumbling campaign gained its footing. He came within a point of overtaking Nixon's post-Labor Day lead of 15 percent.

These conflicting pressures surfaced more than two years earlier when Humphrey was invited by the *C&C* board to be the principal speaker at the journal's twenty-fifth anniversary celebration in New York City. Humphrey knew that many of his recently disaffected allies would be in attendance. How the audience would react could not be predicted with assurance. I can say that the inside job of convincing the Humphrey scheduling staff that the Vice President should accept was very difficult. Why send the V.P. up to New York just to be embarrassed? What possible benefit can this speech be to Humphrey?

It was a tough sell up until the moment that Humphrey realized the ceremony was also going to honor his longtime friend from the Americans for Democratic Action, the theologian Reinhold Niebuhr. Niebuhr had not been well in recent months. Humphrey was not someone who would stand up an old friend struggling with health problems. "I'm not about to say no to Reinie," Humphrey proclaimed. "I am going to New York and this discussion is over."

I recruited William Lee Miller, highly respected author of *The Protestant and Politics*, to prepare draft remarks that I edited slightly. Humphrey worked them over pretty well and, of course, inserted a number of extemporaneous thoughts as he delivered the text. Just back from a lengthy inspection trip to Vietnam, Humphrey charged up to the Riverside Church to do his best, regardless of what might happen. Wayne Cowan, *C&C* editor, provided a firsthand report for *C&C* readers, along with excerpts of Humphrey's speech that are reprinted here.

A TRIBUTE TO REINHOLD NIEBUHR

HUBERT H. HUMPHREY

C&C – May 30, 1966

COMMENTS BY WAYNE H. COWAN

We regret that Mr. Humphrey's speech was too long to print in its entirety. The full text, accompanied by photographs of the occasion, is available in a booklet obtainable from the Vice President's office in Washington, D. C.

No other item on the day's agenda produced quite so much anxiety and excitement as did the scheduled appearance of the Vice President. The world situation had changed considerably following the issuance of the invitation, and both the hosts and the guest found themselves in the anomalous position of disagreeing on a question of major proportions— the war in Vietnam.

The anxiety arose largely over the question of whether the Vice President would return from Vietnam in time for the celebration. As it happened he arrived in the States with barely enough time to brief the President and Congressional leaders before coming to New York. Tired as he was after his 49,025-mile, sixteen-day trip, he insisted on keeping his date to pay tribute to his longtime friend, Reinhold Niebuhr. On the way to the banquet he visited Dr. and Mrs. Niebuhr, who were prevented from attending by Dr. Niebuhr's ill health.

The excitement grew particularly from the fact that there was bound to be a confrontation on Vietnam at a high level since this was Mr. Humphrey's first public appearance after his return. He was preceded at the microphone by Prof. Hans Morgenthau, who both paid tribute to Dr. Niebuhr and attacked the Administration's policy in Vietnam, and by

Dr. John C. Bennett, who, after speaking of Dr. Niebuhr's role in the journal, enumerated many of the positions taken by it through the years and concluded by reading from the jointly signed editorial, "We Protest the National Policy in Vietnam," in the March 7 issue. By the time Toastmaster Roger L. Shinn introduced Congressman John Brademas, who presented the Vice President, the air fairly tingled with tension.

One writer described it this way: "When at last Mr. Humphrey, who had sat listening to all this, got up to speak, most of the audience stood to applaud, but a noticeable few remained grimly seated. It cannot be said that in this difficult situation Mr. Humphrey won over the hostile part of the audience. His opening spontaneous remarks were as ebullient and humorous as ever and very effective. But when he got to the Vietnam section of his speech, he reiterated phrases about 'aggression' that did not convince the unconvinced in this particular group" (William Lee Miller in Presbyterian Life, *April 1 issue).*

Nevertheless, when the Vice President's speech was finished, the applause indicated that not even Vietnam could take away the high esteem in which Hubert Humphrey was held by most of the audience.

REMARKS BY VICE PRESIDENT HUMPHREY

WE ALL KNOW that to speak of *Christianity and Crisis* is to speak of Reinhold Niebuhr, our good friend. It is with this deep sense of privilege and humility that I join this very distinguished assemblage tonight in honoring one of America's and, I think, one of the world's most profound political philosophers, scholars, theologians and prophets. . . .

The Nineteen Twenties and the first two or three years of the Thirties were pretty empty years in American intellectual and political life. It was in this moral vacuum that a new voice was heard, the voice of an unknown preacher serving a working-class community in Detroit. And ever since that time Reinhold Niebuhr has been taming the cynics and pulling Utopians back to earth. No preacher or teacher, at least in my time, has had a greater impact on the secular world. No American has made a greater contribution to political wisdom and moral responsibility.

Reinhold Niebuhr, like Abraham Lincoln and Mark Twain, came out of that great middle western river valley and he brought east with him his realism, his humor, his energy and a brooding thoughtfulness. Like Lincoln and Mark Twain, Dr. Niebuhr brought a mixture of profundity and practicality. Like Lincoln . . . he showed how to combine decisive action with a sensitive knowledge of the complexity of life, including politics.

That combination is what he taught to a whole generation of us as we came out of the Great Depression. We knew there were urgent demands of social justice that required direct action and idealism. At the same time, we had learned that politics was complicated and many-sided, that life just wasn't simple. Dr. Niebuhr was the man more than any other who put these two things together and showed how they are both connected with our religious faith. Yes, he helped us to see that politicians and theologians had a mutual interest in sin and evil in the world.

Martin Luther, I believe, once noted that the state was ordained by God because of man's sin—and the function of a state was to restrain evil-doers. Now if these words sound a bit old-fashioned and fundamentalist, I can assure you that when I was the Mayor of the City of Minneapolis, one of my main jobs was to do just that—restrain evildoers.

James Madison expressed the same proposition in somewhat different and possibly more refined words in *The Federalist*. He said, "If men were angels, no government would be necessary." Well, the vocation of the politician includes the task of dealing with the fallen angels and of mitigating man's inhumanity to man. In positive terms then, our task is to create or to help to create the external conditions for social justice and for human dignity and for freedom. But we must, I am sorry to suggest, be willing to accept man as he is, not as we want him to be, to work with the material at hand. And this is surely at the core of our democratic faith and democratic institutions. . . .

In scores of books and hundreds of articles . . . Reinie has hammered away at this basic theme: "Man's capacity for justice makes democracy possible, but man's inclination to injustice makes democracy necessary." . . . he has asserted his belief in the upper reaches of human nature, in what he called "original righteousness"; man is made in the image of God and, at his best, is capable of justice. . . . At the same time he has affirmed what we all know, that all men, including good men, have a tendency to pursue their private ambitions and interests, often to the detriment of the rights and interests of their fellowman. . . .

So after the rhetoric is over, the case for democracy must rest on its realism: democracy takes into account the full range of human nature, not the perfect man, not the imperfect man, but man. It is the only form of government that can guarantee both justice and freedom, because it is the only one that seeks to recognize and respect the legitimate claims of all conflicting interests. With these insights into human nature and the human condition, our friend Dr. Niebuhr helped many of us understand our obligation to work for social justice without falling into soft Utopian nonsense.

These were the essential truths that my generation of Americans had to hear, and he spoke to us clearly and courageously. Yes, he was not only a man of thought but of action, of political action. It was this commitment to philosophy and action that led him to spearhead, along with some of the rest of us, the formation of Americans for Democratic Action (ADA). Yes, and the Liberal Party, too!

In sum, then, Reinhold Niebuhr has contributed to American life and thought because he has been a realist without despair, an idealist without illusion. But I believe that his wisdom should be heard by other generations as well, by the social activists of today, by the young

Left—the students—the clergy and the civil rights workers who are speaking out with such conviction and courage.

I for one applaud much of what they are doing . . . [and] I know there has been a new burst of social idealism. . . . One of the many side benefits of the civil rights movement is this new social conscience. In fact, I think it is a testimonial to this nation that at the moment of its greatest wealth, it is concerned about the poor and about poverty. But sometimes it occurs to me that the new generation of students and clergy might also need to sit at the feet of this great human being as many of us certainly did in the Thirties and Forties and Fifties.

The great tradition of social protest in America, and a noble tradition it is, . . . has failings that crop up regularly; and I think we ought to talk about them since we are among friends. One is oversimplification and another is a tendency toward self-righteousness. But if you have to make a choice, it is better to oversimplify. Another is just being politically naive. And another is sweeping impatience with everybody in authority. The establishment and the power structure is what they are now called; we had other names in my younger days, but they meant the same. I think we talked about the system . . . .

Reinhold Niebuhr demonstrated for us as he demonstrates for the young social reformer today the vital need for self-criticism, self-analysis, criticism of humane movements by those who believe in their purposes. And one aspect of this liberal self-criticism is to understand the limits of politics. Many idealists picture what ought to be without enough attention to what can be. I would hope and pray that every person who has a noble thought of humanitarianism will read the life of Abraham Lincoln—a man revered today for his idealism and his humanitarianism who was yet the most prudent and able politician in American history. He moved cautiously.

Many idealists do not put themselves in the place of responsible officials who try to imagine what is possible and what isn't possible. I think it was Franklin Roosevelt who once said that he made little compromises in order to be in a position to make great decisions. To Roosevelt a compromise was not a sellout, it was a maneuver to win a battle.

On one occasion Dr. Niebuhr illustrated this point by quoting the passage that Stephen Vincent Benet gives to Abraham Lincoln. I know that most of you here tonight have heard it and read it. Here's what Stephen Vincent Benet said:

> *They come to me and talk about God's will*
> *In righteous deputations and platoons,*
> *Day after day, laymen and ministers.*
> *They write me Prayers from Twenty Million Souls*
> *Defining me God's will and Horace Greeley's.*
> *God's will is General This and Senator That,*
> *God's will is those poor colored fellows' will,*
> *It is the will of the Chicago churches,*
> *It is this man's and his worst enemy's.*
> *But all of them are sure they know God's will.*
> *I am the only man who does not know it.*

Now one thing about our good friend Reinhold Niebuhr is that he has never claimed to know God's will, but he has understood the importance of preserving in America the great liberal and humanitarian objectives we derive from our Anglo-Saxon heritage—the rule of law, consent of the governed and fair play. And he has understood why this nation must be committed to the great Judeo-Christian values of human dignity and equality of opportunity and the dream of a better and more just society. He has been both a reformer and a prophet, but he has not been a crusader. He has steadfastly warned against the nostrum peddler and the salesman of simple solutions and the fixer, all of whom promise easy answers at bargain prices.

Yes, Dr. Niebuhr has always understood there is no easy way out of difficult dilemmas because there is no escape from human situations. There is no painless remedy for racial prejudice and injustice, which still exist in America, no quick or easy victory in the war on poverty, no simple solution to the complex tragic situation facing America in Southeast Asia. These are all complex matters, and none of them is solved by emotion or even demonstration. The challenge is to recognize and accept the complexity and difficulties of these tasks, yet nevertheless to face them in the knowledge that they cannot be evaded. In the words of Keats, "to bear all naked truths, and to envisage circumstance, all calm. . . ." To do it with reason, dialogue, conversation and with conviction. . . .

May I be permitted this final observation on the twenty-fifth anniversary of *Christianity and Crisis*? These have been twenty-five productive and challenging years. . . . They have been years true to the original vision and purpose of Reinhold Niebuhr and the other founders of this Christian journal of opinion.

What of the future? I hope that *Christianity and Crisis* will continue publishing for another quarter of a century. I hope to be around to read it that long and for many years beyond that. We are going to need it very much in the years ahead because it is an honest journal and its opinions are expressed with a basic sense of integrity. We are going to need it because two things are not going to go away: the claims of social justice and the complexity of politics . . . such journals as this stimulate the critical faculties of both our leaders and our citizens . . . I have every confidence that its unwavering commitment to social justice, to honest and perceptive controversy and its profound understanding of the intricacies of the democratic process will provide ample copy for years to come. . . .

Christianity and Crisis, as a Christian journal, must by definition have a perspective as wide as humankind and one eye on eternity. It cannot afford to reflect parochial nationalism or a short-run outlook. A journal like that, a perspective like that, is the requirement of our time.

. . . I, as well as many others who honor you on this important birthday, expect you to live up to your reputation. And your reputation is that of a publication that seeks not to tell men what to think but above all tries to arouse in them the desire to think—to think profoundly—to think not only of the present but of the tomorrows.

"STIRRINGS OF THE DREAM"

An unsolicited piece—"Stirrings of the Dream"—that I wrote in March 1973 for *The New Yorker* magazine provides an interesting coda to the events of the 1960s that I comment upon in the preceding pages. Not surprisingly, my unsolicited manuscript did not fit with *The New Yorker*'s "editorial plans" to quote from the rejection letter, but it did give me an opportunity to ponder what really happened in that tumultuous decade and where we, as a nation, might realistically head in its aftermath. I filed the rejected manuscript away and promptly forgot about it.

Thirty years later—in 2003—while going through my files of civil rights documents at the request of Robert Caro, prize-winning biographer of Lyndon Johnson and Robert Moses, I unearthed "Stirrings of the Dream." As with my articles from *C&C*, I found what I had to say interesting and instructive, at least in contrast to our current domestic political and legislative environment. From the perspective of this volume, it also provided a useful overview of the remarkable advances—and also the shortcomings—in civil rights and racial justice that took place in mid-century America, as well as a look at many of the major personalities who made these things happen. Here were the people who crossed over to the Promised Land in the mid-1960s, however briefly. This piece also provided me with an opportunity to preview many of the themes and arguments that I subsequently would make in my book, *One Last Chance: the Democratic Party, 1974–1976*. Much of what I had to say then, some thirty years ago, still rings true today. I commend my thoughts to fellow Democrats seeking to recover from the latest electoral debacle.

Finally, as it turned out, the events at the LBJ Library described in "Stirrings of the Dream" constituted the last public event in Lyndon Johnson's extraordinary life. He died five weeks later. Less than two years later, the political life of Richard Nixon also came to an end as he resigned the office of President on August 9, 1974. The strategies being contemplated by Humphrey and others, as described in the manuscript, to reach out to President Nixon in support of continued racial progress quickly became irrelevant as the scandal that came to be known as Watergate inexorably unfolded. Not even Humphrey's irrepressible determination to recapture the momentum of the 1960s in support of racial progress—to reach out again for the Promised Land—could overcome that earthshaking political and constitutional crisis.

STIRRINGS OF THE DREAM
March 1973

I went along for the ride.

Back in the early 1960s, I had worked for Hubert Humphrey during his first senatorial incarnation and at a time when he had as much as anybody to do with what happened in the United States Senate.

As his legislative assistant, I witnessed one of the few legislative miracles of this generation, the passage of the Civil Rights Act of 1964. And I acquired that mid-1960s sense of optimism and faith in the good works of good men that arose from this and other legislative victories.

So Humphrey invited me to go along to the Civil Rights Symposium arranged by the Lyndon Baines Johnson Library and the University of Texas on the occasion of the opening of LBJ's civil rights papers. A two-day program had been arranged, including many of the giants of the civil rights movement, as it used to be called.

Retired Chief Justice Earl Warren would make one of his infrequent public appearances and deliver the keynote. Humphrey would make a speech. And so would a man who had almost vanished from the American political scene, Lyndon B. Johnson.

The event had all the earmarks of a class reunion of people who, a decade ago, had seemingly mastered the art of governing this country only to discover one day that everything had gone wrong. They had been unceremoniously cast out of office, their achievements in large measure condemned, their reputations for enlightened and humane leadership badly tarnished.

And, the unkindest cut of all, their self-assured optimism about the perfection of this society had been replaced among the people by a profound and cynical mistrust of popular government, of political leaders, and of the democratic system itself which they had glorified in their years of power.

These were the people, most now out of government, who reserved two days in December to meet again with Lyndon Johnson and, one would suppose, to look backwards.

True, the letter of invitation from Harry Middleton, the director of the LBJ Library, had said that " . . . the purpose of the symposium will be not to look back, but rather to look ahead to see what this nation should be doing to fulfill its commitments in the decade ahead." But the roster of invited guests and the participation of LBJ himself seemed to suggest another course, another direction.

But that is not what happened.

• • •

Braniff's flight 11 to Austin was scheduled to depart Washington's Dulles Airport at 5:30 P.M. on Sunday, December 10. Coming around the last turn of the limited access road that links the airport to Washington's freeway system, one was struck once again by the sheer, breathtaking grandeur of Eero Saarinen's masterpiece as it was silhouetted by the sunset. It forced a momentary thought: What unlikely combination of political and artistic forces made it possible? Or was it just luck?

I was to meet Humphrey at the airport. Since his schedule is apt to be erratic even in the most normal circumstances, I thought it wise to arrive early and wait.

It is not often that you walk up to a line of people at an airport and know personally fourteen of the seventeen people who are ahead of you. Faces, names, people I had not seen for years, in many cases, and who had neither seen nor heard from me in a similar period. The momentary panic of the forgotten name, by both parties, covered over with the, "Well, how are you? What are you doing now?"

The honest joy of reunion was tempered by the shared embarassment of our common heritage: in the main, a group of Democrats (the
great Republican Chief Justice excepted) far removed from the seats of
power come together to celebrate victories that most people now took
for granted or had forgotten.

Harry McPherson, one of LBJ's most respected assistants, now a
Washington attorney, a good friend, looked up and smiled a puckish
smile. "Isn't it wonderful how much we did for these folks ten years
ago?" he said.

That was it, the self-conscious humor of people sufficiently honest
to see the political irrelevancy of the gathering, yet honestly pleased to
see friends and allies who had disappeared for years, even in the narrow confines of the politically active in Washington, D.C. And now
everyone was headed to the LBJ Library in Austin.

The whole enterprise seemed to symbolize the hollowness of our
contemporary understanding of the country and its problems, the sim-
plicity of our earlier faith in a democratic process now mired in
cynicism, and the absence of our vision of what the Democratic Party
should become in the aftermath of the McGovern debacle.

Many of us laughed quietly to ourselves, even as we recognized the
uniqueness of the event itself. We had not been together for years and
now we were. We could enjoy that, even if we could not take the event
itself seriously. Having known power, or been close to power, we
could not mistake a social occasion for something political.

• • •

The mobile lounge filled up and moved out to the waiting Braniff
plane that had come from New York.

Harry McPherson, an early supporter of Edmund Muskie for the
Democratic nomination, was describing his principal contribution to
the McGovern campaign.

It seemed that one day Gary Hart, one of the more prominent McGovern campaign directors, called McPherson to ask if he would direct a presidential transition task force that would plan the transfer of authority from the Nixon to the McGovern administration. Since McGovern, at the time, was holding steady at a 30 point deficit in the public opinion polls, McPherson inquired of the seriousness of the request. It was totally serious. McPherson then asked for guidance about what he should tell persons who might be asked to join the planning group.

"What should I say when they laugh?" he asked.

The message from Hart was clear: tell them they laughed in the primaries, too. McGovern is going to win.

And the recommendations were to be completed before Election Day.

"Well," McPherson continued, "I called Clark Clifford to ask his advice since he had been in overall charge of the Kennedy transition. He said that I could look at any of the documents from that period but, first, I ought to know that Senator McGovern on a recent news interview program had announced that he, Clifford, and Ted Sorensen had been put in charge of the transition project."

McPherson went on to describe the series of phone calls that then ensued between himself and various members of the McGovern staff.

Yes, McGovern had met Sorenson at a fundraising party in New York and, on the spot, asked him to direct the transition with Clifford. No, there was little sense in McPherson, Clifford and Sorensen doing the same thing.

A compromise, of sorts, was eventually worked out: Clifford would work on substantive issues; McPherson would take charge of recruiting personnel for the new administration. It was not clear what Sorensen's assignment would turn out to be. And all of this taking place in the context of Nixon leading nearly every poll by a two to one margin. The story epitomized the make-believe quality that infused so much of the McGovern presidential campaign from its beginnings in

Miami Beach. It also said something about what had happened to the Democratic Party.

More people going to the symposium were on the plane from New York. I found myself sitting next to Ralph Ellison, the black writer, who decided to make the trip when LBJ wired him personally. "I've never said no to the President and I'm not about to start now," Ellison said.

The politicians among us, both elected and natural, had some trouble sitting down. Each time they tried, a new face would compel a sprint down the aisle, a handshake, an embrace, a hurried conversation. The plane was about to take off and the stewardesses were forced to take stronger measures.

"Would Mr. Valenti please take his seat or the plane will not be permitted to take off," said the voice on the public address system. Cheers and applause.

"Thank you, David Halberstam," whooped Jack Valenti, the most loyal of LBJ assistants and now president of the Motion Picture Association.

I reminded Ralph Ellison that we had last talked in December 1967 when I invited him to accompany Vice President Humphrey on his good-will trip to Africa. Ellison had declined because his house had just burned and manuscripts had been destroyed in the fire. It was no time to go to Africa.

"You're writing something, I'm sure," I said.

"Yes, a novel. It's almost finished. I've got to sit down with my editor very soon and see where we are."

"I assume you don't like to talk about it with strangers," I said.

"You assume correctly," Ellison replied.

And then he began to talk about the presidential campaign and the Democratic Party.

"What is this business with the Democrats? What is this self-righteous preaching we've heard for the last year? Don't you understand the stakes in all of this?

"That man who is dying in a Kansas City hospital, the man we are going to honor in Texas, they understood their responsibilities. They saw their duty as winning political power so that they could have an impact on people's lives. I finally concluded the Democrats deserved to lose this year.

"Truman, he understood," Ellison continued. "He was an artillery captain in World War I and he saw segregation firsthand. He saw the black regiments in Europe. And as soon as he had a chance to change it, he did.

"He took on McArthur, a man who seemed to many people as superior to Truman. But Truman knew the uses of power and he was not afraid.

"The same with FDR. He never indulged in self-righteous notions that would deny him the power he needed to get the job done.

"The Democratic Party must be an instrument for resolving the bitter conflicts in this country. That's its major reason for being.

"But that requires a Democrat in the White House."

Ellison talked at length about his early years in Oklahoma, about how, in the midst of a totally segregated society, he came to love this country and its people.

"I spent a lot of time in the local drug store, all black, and I listened to the men talking. Sophisticated political talk, about their problems and their hopes. There was an honesty and a realism there that has never left me. I've never known the luxury of being holier-than-thou.

"Take Humphrey back there, another druggist, he's the same way."

He looked around the plane. Andrew Brimmer, governor of the Federal Reserve System, black, born to a poor Louisiana family, walked down the aisle.

"Just look at the people on this plane. Where they've come from, what they've done with their lives. What a wonderful country."

About a half-hour from Austin, the pilot reported that freezing rain had made it impossible to land and that we would head for San

Antonio, hopefully to land there. Buses would be waiting to take us back to Austin.

Nobody seemed to mind.

In the San Antonio airport the scramble for luggage occupied most people. Humphrey, however, charged into the coffee shop to shake some hands.

And we all exchanged the predictable one-liner: "Here we are, on our way to LBJ's civil rights symposium, being bussed across Texas with Vernon Jordan, Clarence Mitchell, Hubert Humphrey and . . . Earl Warren."

On the bus I sat next to John Macy, head of the Civil Service Commission under Johnson, and recently resigned—under administration pressure—as president of the Corporation for Public Broadcasting.

His mood was somber, not only in regard to the recently-visible administration attacks against a number of public affairs programs supported by CPB but, more generally, in relation to the growing politicization of the entire civil service.

"The career service is being damaged severely, not to mention the many individual cases of good people who are simply removed or shifted into meaningless jobs This is the kind of damage that takes decades to repair," he said.

Macy wondered further how the White House would function in Nixon's second term.

"Now that his reelection is no longer the single goal around which to make decisions, how will they judge their actions? How will they know what to do?"

We finally arrived in Austin, after a slow tortuous crawl along Interstate 35. As we unloaded the busses at the Sheraton motel, I had my chance. I saved Earl Warren's luggage from the innermost recesses of the baggage compartment as the bus was about to leave for its next stop.

Just another example of the trouble you cause when you start bussing people around.

...

Freezing rain was still falling the next morning. The local segment on the CBS Morning News was a non-stop recitation of school closings and highway problems. Not a word about the symposium, even though Lady Bird Johnson owned the station.

Cars and busses slithered off toward the East Campus auditorium, an attractive facility seating about 1,000 people and located in the same building as the Lyndon B. Johnson School of Government. Across a stone plaza loomed the LBJ Library, about ten stories tall, solid stone side walls, with a row of windows at the very top. LBJ's helicopter can land on the roof and his office is said to have a commanding view of the football stadium. It's Longhorn country.

The auditorium was about half-full when we arrived; students, faculty, invited guests settling down for a long day. A small contingent from the Longhorn Band was performing in the front. Those participants fortunate enough to have triumphed over the weather were gathering in the green room behind the stage. Lady Bird was there, greeting the guests, making everyone feel welcome. LBJ reportedly was on his way from the ranch.

The program got underway about a half-hour late, even though LBJ still hadn't arrived. After the usual welcoming remarks by the University president and others, Patricia Roberts Harris, the black former dean of Howard University Law School and chairman of the Credentials Committee of the 1972 Democratic National Convention, introduced the Chief Justice.

"We have known for some time that civil rights was facing an icy reception, but seldom has it been so graphically illustrated as today," she observed.

Then she got down to business.

" . . . The present day justification of treatment of the legitimate continuing aspirations of black Americans reminds me of the scene from George Orwell's *1984* in which the protagonist sits before a computer and corrects back issues of newspapers and reports to conform these primary sources of history to immediate demands of the holders of power. If the facts did not support the position taken by the government, the government simply changed the facts," she said.

"We have no reason to believe that double-think and newspeak have reached this country in the form described by Orwell, but there are trends that are frighteningly similar . . .

"Allegations of the historic primacy of the neighborhood school and the assertions of recency of the use of the school bus are egregious examples of the rewriting of history for present policy purposes . . .

"The documentation of the Johnson era to be found in this library will serve to refute the post hoc suggestions that the Johnson period promised 'too much' or 'more than could be delivered,' as has been asserted by some white reactionaries, conservatives, and to my surprised regret, liberals in the attempts of the past four years either to ignore or to rewrite the history of the period from November 1963 to January 1969 . . ."

Patricia Harris had touched the heart of the matter. The absence of direction in the country, no less than the absence of direction and purpose in the Democratic Party, could be seen, in part, as a product of the savage attacks that had been leveled against the record of the Johnson years, a massive rewriting of what Pat Harris termed the "reality of the role of the Johnson administration in the elimination of legally enforced racial segregation, and in leading the people of the United States to accept the right of every black American both to aspire to and to receive all the benefits, prestige and status available to whites."

The Vietnam War, of course, was the triggering mechanism for this rewriting. And few people, at this juncture, would argue that the manifold costs of America's escalation of and participation in this conflict were remotely justified. But the indictment could not end there; it had to be far more encompassing, covering most of the Johnson record—domestic and foreign—of those years.

Those who participated in the rewriting—the Orwellians of the late 1960s and early 1970s—were found in both political parties and across the ideological spectrum. Democratic practitioners of the "new politics" seemed unable to accept or comprehend positive social achievement from the man who led us into Indochina. Nixonites, sensing the Democratic vulnerability arising from the massive upheavals within the party, joined the attack, with different rhetoric and different objectives but, in the end, with the same result of distorting the truth for their own ends.

This kind of pincer movement naturally produced the conventional wisdom that was accepted by nearly everybody who knew anything about politics: the Great Society had failed dismally, not only because of the Vietnam War but, more fundamentally, because it over-promised, over-centralized, and over-burdened an exhausted and dispirited people.

The Orwellian strategy worked—the "new politics" prevailed, to a degree, within the Democratic Party and the Nixonites walked off with the government—but not without a price. Tampering with history can be dangerous, especially among a people who, until very recently, have taken considerable pride in their national achievements and who have grounded their future aspirations on the foundation of this historical reality. We had some notion of where we, as a people, were heading because we shared some common perceptions about whence we had come. Attack these foundations, destroy these guideposts, and the present becomes far more ominous and foreboding. People and nations lose their vision. Political parties sacrifice their sense of identity and purpose.

That the conventional wisdom was believed, even by many of those whom it indicted, had been demonstrated the previous evening at Dulles Airport. The self-conscious gathering of people a decade out of date, to celebrate events that we had been led to believe ought not to be celebrated, resulted in the good-humored embarassment at the Braniff counter.

Pat Harris herself was not exempt. Before her introductory remarks, I had asked of her feelings about the symposium. She replied: "This looks more like a wake than anything else. This is all just about a decade late."

But she, more than most, knew better. And when she got up to present the Chief Justice, she proved it. She remembered without apology.

So did Earl Warren.

He delivered a thorough and stirring account of America's continuing struggle to make equality under law more than a promise in the Declaration of Independence. He traced the legal origins of slavery, the congressional civil rights initiatives following the Civil War, the destruction of these rights by the Supreme Court in the closing decades of the 19th century, beginning with the *Slaughter House* and *Civil Rights* cases and concluding with the "separate but equal" doctrine of *Plessy v. Ferguson*. It was this doctrine that produced what Warren described as " . . . a torrent of racist legislation and governmental practices in the Southern states that brought the black people there close to a condition of apartheid in the twenties and thirties of this twentieth century."

He then described, for fully ten minutes, what it was like to be a Southern black around the middle of this century. For those who never knew, or who had forgotten, it was a chilling recitation of suppression and separateness, including every area of life, public and private.

In the 1940s and 1950s, the three branches of the Federal government began, slowly but steadily, to remedy these injustices, culminating in the Supreme Court's disapproval of the "separate but equal" doctrine in *Brown v. Board of Education* and in the civil rights legislation of the late 1950s and the 1960s.

Warren concluded with what could only be described, and was by the press in attendance, as words of admonition for President Nixon:

"We will either go forward to our announced goal of proving that all men are created equal and, as such, are entitled to life, liberty, and the pursuit of happiness, or we will denigrate the plural society we envisioned and developed, and revert to a 'house divided' which the prophetic Lincoln said 'cannot stand.' We have suffered greatly from such divisiveness, and it would be well for those who are obstinate, or timid, or thoughtless to remember the admonition that those who fail to learn the lessons of history are destined to relive them . . .

"All laws are ineffective unless there is a will on the part of those in authority to enforce them, and a leadership in them to inspire the people who must eventually pay the price of a society disrupted from any cause to obey the law because it is in the interest of all."

The cumulative impact of Warren's words was remarkable. He brought back to life the enormity of the wrong that had left 20 million Americans as near outcasts in their own country, and the extraordinary governmental feat that had demolished, in a little more than two decades, the legal basis for this wrong. The drama was heightened by the arrival of Lyndon Johnson, midway through the Chief Justice's remarks.

His reported poor health and the near-impassable roads around Austin had not succeeded in keeping LBJ at the ranch. He was here, looking surprisingly well, and ready to take part from start to finish.

Instead of rewriting history, the day had begun with a spirited effort to recapture it and, perhaps, in so doing, to lay the groundwork for a more precise sense of the future.

■ ■ ■

The program originally called for Roy Wilkins, executive director of the NAACP, to speak after Warren on "The Record of the 1960s." Again the weather intervened, delaying Wilkins' arrival until mid-afternoon. Escorted into the auditorium by LBJ, directed by LBJ to sit in his seat in the front row, Wilkins symbolized the antithesis of those who would emulate Orwell's protagonist, for whatever motive, in restructuring the events of the past decade.

He, too, remembered without apology. His speech was simple and straightforward, describing the 1960s as "a time of significant history;" the history of the sit-ins and freedom rides, the Birmingham demonstrations, the assassination of Medgar Evars—the first of many civil rights leaders who would be struck down in this decade—the murder by bombing of four young black girls in a Birmingham church, the March on Washington, the legislative victories and the murders of John F. Kennedy, Martin Luther King, and Robert F. Kennedy.

It was not his words that spoke most eloquently, but his presence and demeanor. At one moment, seemingly a voice from the past and little more, old, almost tired, occasionally stumbling in his delivery. But the fires still burned in his eyes, the good humor bubbled up, a quiet man, yet secure in himself and in his life. He felt little need to convince us of what had taken place in these years: the facts spoke for themselves, without embellishment and exaggeration. The Orwellians were beneath contempt.

Due to the last-minute change in schedule, Wilkins was preceded in the morning by Vernon Jordan, the young successor to Whitney Young as executive director of the National Urban League, and by Hubert Humphrey. To the extent that a structure existed to the program, Warren and Wilkins were supposed to recount the historical record; everybody else had the general assignment of looking to the future.

Jordan sketched out the new dimensions of civil rights concerns in the aftermath of the advances of the 1960s, or, as he called it, the Second Reconstruction:

"In the sixties, the issue was the right to sit on the bus; today the issue is where that bus is going and what does it cost to get there. In the sixties, the issue was the right to eat at the lunch counter; today the issue is the hunger and malnutrition that stalk the land. In the sixties, the issue was fair employment opportunity. Today, that can no longer be separated from full employment of black people and equal access to every kind and level of employment, up to and including top policy-making jobs.

" . . . The strategies black people and committed white people must develop in the seventies will revolve around issues like revenue sharing, metropolitan government, and internal regulations of Federal and state regulatory agencies. The battleground has shifted from the streets where people marched to end segregation on busses, to the computer rooms where analysts will have to examine data on bus routes, on where black people live and where they travel to work, and on alternate rate structures that will make riding cheaper for poor people.

" . . . It means that the civil rights movement, which has shown its excellence as a legal and moral force, and as a marching and pressure movement, will have to deal with the complexities of power as it never had to in the sixties, when the President was a friend of the movement and the villains were clearly identifiable sheriffs whose snapping police dogs and vicious cattle prods won us headlines and friends.

"So civil rights in the seventies will be less dramatic and less popular. It will be an era of trench warfare, requiring knowledgeable technicians skillfully monitoring and exposing racism in the twilight zone of America's institutional policymaking processes . . . "

Humphrey, exuberant as ever, followed Jordan to the podium and seemed ready to lead the multitudes into the trenches right then and there. There was a hard-headed bluntness about his words that has often been lacking in his more unversalistic calls to expunge evil and human misery wherever extant.

"I begin with this proposition," said Humphrey. "Unless we agree on a strategy that can attract a majority coalition in the Congress and the nation at large, we can look forward to little in the way of concrete results. This lesson is as true today as it was twenty years ago.

"Between the two extremes of empty appeals to the nation's moral consciousness and to premeditated violence and intimidation lies a broad field for constructive political action. And it is in this area where we must begin to think more creatively."

Recalling the seventy-five-day struggle to break the Southern filibuster and pass the Civil Rights Act of 1964, Humphrey noted that " . . . our eventual triumph was not pre-ordained, by any means. At numerous points . . . the legislation could have been compromised irretrievably. The fact that none of this happened was due almost entirely to the political strategy that had been mapped out and that was followed even in the most difficult moments of the debate.

" . . . The struggle for civil rights in Congress has never been easy and, in many respects, our present difficulties are no more insuperable than the barriers we faced back in the good old days. Different, to be sure, but not insuperable."

Out of the tangled mess of the 1972 presidential campaign came several clues to a political strategy that Humphrey thought might eventually produce a working majority in Congress to back the kind of national initiatives that would give life to Vernon Jordan's new civil rights agenda.

First, argued Humphrey, the civil rights movement could no longer base its strategy on the notion of a "special break" for blacks or other minorities.

"Any political appeal that appears, rightly or wrongly, as favoring one group or class of people over another is going to be rejected by a majority of the American electorate."

To Humphrey this simply meant expanding the appeal and broadening the base. "What is needed," he said, "is the creation of a climate of identity between the needs—the hopes and fears—of the minorities and the needs—the hopes and fears—of the majority."

Second, the 1972 presidential election suggested that this objective might not be as unattainable as the conventional wisdom would suggest. Despite George McGovern's disastrous personal showing, certain of the issues that he advocated—tax reform and cutting excessive defense spending, for example—still attract significant national support.

"Progress in these two areas . . . would begin to provide the Federal government with the financial resources that are essential in any realistic attack on our most urgent domestic problems . . . There is virtually no segment of our society that would not benefit directly from meaningful progress in each of these areas," Humphrey said.

Third, President Nixon's landslide victory placed within his grasp an extraordinary opportunity to move to the forefront of the nation's quest for racial progress in the 1970s. Humphrey pointed out that such presidential initiative would be no more surprising than his trips to China and Russia and his adoption of wage and price controls. And, then, a President in his second term begins to ponder the judgments of history.

"And I can imagine no more harsh indictment than his having failed to lead the United States in the most critical and urgent area of domestic concern.

"Such a move," Humphrey said, "would be supported and applauded by the large majority of Democrats and, I suspect, by a significant number of Republicans. It would bring back to life, almost overnight, the bipartisan coalition that was responsible for all the civil rights legislation of the 1960s."

...

A former President, who had helped create and sustain this coalition of Democrats and Republicans because it was the only way a civil rights bill could pass in the Senate, seemed to be enjoying himself immensely. After hearing reports for months of LBJ's poor health, his lack of energy, and his near hermit-like existence at the ranch, most people assumed that last minute regrets would be delivered by Lady Bird. And so Lyndon Johnson's arrival during Warren's keynote address produced surprise and some excitement among the audience.

Dressed in a brown, Texas-style suit with boots, Lyndon Johnson sat at one end of the front row of seats in the audience and immediately assumed the pose that White House photographer Okamoto caught many times: leaning forward, chin cupped by his right hand, right elbow on right knee. Movie and still photographers jammed together in the corner of their assigned area and shot steadily for the next quarter hour.

Johnson looked good. The long white hair that had been evident in the photographs of his meeting with George McGovern early in the campaign had been sheared off. His face was well tanned and betrayed little trace of the physical exhaustion that accompanies heart attacks.

He listened intently to Warren's words, exhibited no reaction at the several points where the audience applauded the Chief Justice's favorable remarks about Johnson's legislative and executive actions in behalf of civil rights, and, at the conclusion of the speech, walked up the steps to the podium, embraced Warren, and escorted him back to an adjacent seat in the front row. And so it went, through the morning's program, LBJ displaying great interest in the speeches and no apparent reaction to the accolades that were heaped around him.

During the recess for lunch—Texas barbecue, what else?—LBJ made the rounds among the guests and participants, much as he used to prowl the Senate floor as majority leader. Now he was much heavier than in the 1950s and walked more slowly, but he had not lost the ability to cover the ground and touch all the bases: a hand shake, a greeting, a whispered word or two, and on to the next person.

There was, of course, an important difference: in the 1950s Lyndon Johnson's sociability on the Senate floor had a definite political purpose; he consciously involved himself in every facet of Senate life—from assigning office space to managing the legislative calendar—using each of these contacts at some future time to perfect one of his intricate legislative stratagems. Now his sociability had no further purpose: he was enjoying the day and he seemed happy that many of his former staff, members of his administration, and political allies were also present.

But if LBJ's reactions were purely social, this was not the case among many of the participants and guests, particularly those from Washington and New York. In talking to my friends who had been on the Braniff flight, I found an almost unanimous feeling about the morning session: what had been perceived initially as a strictly nostalgic experience, pleasant but harmless, had begun to generate an unexpected political focus.

I stopped Pat Harris right before the afternoon session was to begin and complimented her on her presentation of the Chief Justice.

"You know," she said, "I was amazed at how good everybody was. My remark this morning about this being a decade late, well, I'm not so sure at this point. It still makes a difference if you really care. And for the first time in years, nobody seemed ashamed of anything."

It had been refreshing to look back at the civil rights achievements of the past two decades without apology. There had been some tough battles and some important gains had been won. It was a record of which a President and a political party could be proud. It was a foundation on which to build, along the lines suggested by Jordan and Humphrey.

The combination of social idealism and political realism that had produced these gains seemed to offer a basis for beginning, once again, to build a majority coalition in the Congress that could begin to restore some of the lost momentum, not only in the parochial area of civil rights but across a broader spectrum of domestic concerns. The remembrance that this had been done in the fifties and sixties—in a political environment that, initially, was just as inhospitable as the present—had a revitalizing and invigorating effect on everyone with whom I talked.

Three political facts stood out. First, President Nixon had been identified by the three opening speakers as bearing a special burden, and opportunity, in helping this country move forward to the next generation of civil rights advances. Second, these advances, in the main, were tied inextricably to progress on a broad front of domestic issues that potentially could expand their appeal beyond a constituency of "blacks only." Third, the most immediate step was to begin fashioning the outlines of a majority coalition that could push Nixon toward greater effort and could then assist him in winning the battles in Congress.

But this analysis, however attractive it may sound in Austin, Texas, does not get to the heart of the matter: Is this a strategy likely to win the President's support? Is there a base of public attitudes that could be tapped, or is the conventional wisdom correct when it says that most people just want to protect what they have, regardless of the effect this has on society at large?

There is compelling evidence that Richard Nixon is steadfastly opposed to any significant new initiatives on the domestic front. In his widely-quoted interview with Garnett D. Horner of the Washington *Star-News,* Nixon said: " . . . This country has enough on its plate in the way of new spending programs, social programs, throwing dollars at problems. What we need is, basically, reform of existing institutions and not the destruction of our tried values in this country . . . I don't believe that the answer to the nation's problems is simply massive new programs in terms of dollars and in terms of people."

Later in the interview, the President seemed to equate greater Federal effort on the domestic front with the destruction of the individual work ethic in American society: " . . . another thing this election is about is whether we should move toward massive handouts to people, making the people more and more dependent, looking to Government, or whether we say, no, it is up to you. The people are going to have to carry their share of the load.

"The average American is just like the child in the family. You give him some responsibility and he is going to amount to something. He is going to do something. If, on the other hand, you make him completely dependent and pamper him and cater to him too much, you are going to make him soft, spoiled and eventually a very weak individual."

It serves little purpose here to point out that the most pampered person in American society today, the person who carries considerably less than his or her share of the load, is the wealthy, privileged supporter of Richard Nixon who enjoys a tax structure crammed with special advantages totally beyond the reach of the average wage-earner. By the same token, corporations have come to expect a variety of special arrangements, ranging from accelerated depreciation schedules and overseas tax privileges to emergency bail-out procedures backed with government money.

And it is probably fruitless to attempt to grasp the analogy between sensible child-rearing and the Federal government exercising its responsibilities in a number of priority domestic areas, more often than not so designated by the people's representatives in Congress.

But what *is* significant in Nixon's statement, and what bears directly on the issues that were before the symposium, is what appears to be Nixon's conscious effort to muddle the question of governmental action on the domestic front with the notion of governmental hand-outs, give-aways, and the erosion of individual responsibility. To oversimplify only slightly: Mr. Nixon appears to be suggesting that governmental action *per se* equates with welfare and, as everybody knows, welfare means a hand-out, principally for blacks. On the basis of the Nixon analogy, any significant new national commitments in education or housing or health care or whatever fall into the category of a special break for minorities and, presumably, opposed on that basis.

Having sacrificed the traditional Republican anti-spending argument by his record-breaking Federal deficits, Nixon, at least in his *Star-News* interview, seems to have decided on this approach as a replacement—one that plays directly to a significant body of public opinion and, consequently, raises serious doubts about the likelihood of building a coalition based on presidential leadership.

...

Is this, then, the end of the line, at least in terms of the ambitious agenda outlined by Jordan and Humphrey? Or are there reasons to persevere, even in the face of a hostile Presidency?

At this writing, the evidence is ambiguous.

Recent survey research suggests, first of all, the very real political obstacles that have to be overcome in any appeal that focuses primarily on black and other racial minority problems as distinct from the interconnected web of domestic problems generally. In the recent national study of public attitudes, *State of the Nation,* edited by William Watts and Lloyd A. Free, Americans place "the problems of black Americans" in twenty-fourth place out of a ranking of twenty-seven major national issues (rising prices and the cost of living is first;) improving mass transportation systems is twenty-seventh).

Albert H. Cantril and Charles W. Roll, Jr. report that 69 percent of a national sample in May 1972 agreed with the statement: "Blacks and people in other minorities expect things to improve too quickly and are making unreasonable demands."

On the other hand, Watts and Free found considerable national support for a number of specific domestic concerns that affect the lives of blacks and other minorities as much as, if not more than, white Americans. They asked their respondents whether or not they supported increased Federal spending in a number of specific areas.

The results:

	Increased	Present Level	Reduced
"Programs to improve the education of children from low-income families"	62%	28%	3%
"To make a college education possible for young people who could not otherwise afford it"	54%	32%	7%
"Combatting crime"	77%	18%	1%
"Preventing drug abuse"	74%	20%	2%

"To improve medical and health care for Americans generally"	62%	32%	2%
"The Medicaid program to help low-income families pay their medical bills"	52%	35%	6%
"Public Housing"	40%	40%	12%
"Urban Renewal"	51%	29%	11%

These data reveal considerable public support for more vigorous Federal action in a number of specific areas where the Nixon administration reportedly is now planning to hold the line or to cut back the level of Federal expenditures.

But it is significant that as soon as the Federal assistance falls into a category where blacks would seem to be the principal beneficiaries: the level of support for increased spending drops: 40 percent for "public housing" and 51 percent for "urban renewal." Nevertheless, the general public would not appear to share Mr. Nixon's aversion to "throwing money at problems" as long as the toss is directed at a specific and understood problem area.

Cantril and Roll, in their same national survey of May 1972, found that 78 percent of the public agreed with the statement: "The big special interests in this country have too much power and pretty much have their own way." And 72 percent agreed that: "Too few of our nation's leaders understand what the average citizen would like to see done in this country."

The message from these data is relatively unambiguous, at least in terms of measuring the political risks of a strategy based on a "special break" for blacks as opposed to a strategy that sought to attack black problems in the context of a broader offensive against our domestic problems generally. It would appear to confirm Humphrey's proposition that " . . . any political appeal that appears, rightly or wrongly, as favoring one group or class of people over another is going to be rejected by a majority of the American electorate."

But the public support for a variety of Federal domestic initiatives, coupled with the view that national leaders do not understand the problems of the average citizen, holds out some hope of sustaining a coalition that would consciously strive to combine these two sources of political strength.

...

What, then, to do?

The symposium produced no firm decisions on strategy nor were any likely to emerge in a two-day conference, however talented the participants. But there did emerge, I believe, a more sharply defined understanding of the general directions that must now be followed and that, over time, could produce a more specific list of political steps that should be attempted. There also emerged a feeling of self-confidence and pride that had been noticeably absent for the past several years. In the general disarray after the recent presidential election, this was no insignificant accomplishment.

Humphrey reminded the symposium that the absence of presidential support had not proved fatal to the civil rights movement in the past, especially when conscious efforts were made to change the President's mind.

"We forget," Humphrey said, "that the early 1960s was a time of convincing President Kennedy to adopt a more aggressive posture in support of civil rights legislation that had been pending in the Congress for many years. We forget that his initial civil rights proposals in 1963 were judged totally inadequate by the Leadership Conference on Civil Rights. It was only after the dramatic events in Birmingham that the administration became fully committed to the legislative package that eventually became the Civil Rights Act of 1964."

If it is true, as Humphrey suggested, that "Presidents do not operate in a vacuum" then one priority would seem to be the creation of a political environment that would push Mr. Nixon toward greater activism in dealing with the economic and social issues that now comprise both the domestic political agenda and the unfinished business of the civil rights movement. This kind of problem-oriented approach by the Federal government could energize the latent public support that has been documented *if* in the public's mind, these actions are clearly decoupled from programs designed to benefit minority groups only.

A more difficult political task lies in distinguishing between any form of compensatory action and the notion of "quotas." At the moment, there are few more emotionally-laden words loose on the political scene. "Bussing" won more headlines in 1972, but, over the long haul, the potential political effect of quotas is far greater: more of the population is affected more directly, in areas of daily life just as sensitive as elementary and secondary education—jobs, housing, college admissions, governmental contracts, etc. The process of stitching together a majority coalition depends upon achieving some distinction between the broad range of legislatively-sanctioned affirmative action programs and the iron-clad quota arrangements that, quite properly, are an affront and a threat to both whites and blacks.

Vernon Jordan, in his morning address, emphasized this critical distinction: " . . .No one has ever argued in favor of rigid quotas to overcome inequality of opportunity, nor has anyone ever argued in favor of total reliance upon the goodwill and good faith of employers and government agencies.

"Instead, there has been developed a flexible system of guidelines for progress, goals to assure eventual equality of opportunity and timetables to measure progress. When we hear these reasonable mechanisms for insuring success of affirmative action programs labelled as 'quotas' and attacked, we can only conclude that the artificial issue of 'quotas' is yet another wall raised to exclude black people."

The tragedy of Nixon's *Star-News* interview is the President's apparent determination to strengthen these walls of exclusion, just as he seems loath to tap the latent public support for a more energetic assault on our critical domestic problems.

But this need not be a presidential function exclusively. The Democrats in Congress and in the states, the party's major source of strength, have an opportunity to act if they can find the imagination and energy to do so. Thirty-one of the 50 states now have Democratic governors, distributed with rough equality among all sections of the country. Both Houses of Congress are controlled by Democrats and the departure of a number of senior members opens up the legislative system to greater institutional and party activism. Hundreds of cities have Democratic mayors.

These political resources should be put to work in new ways: Democratic members of Congress should travel to the states to meet with governors and mayors, to hold public hearings on specific problems, and the state leaders should be invited regularly to Washington to become direct participants in key legislative battles. The Democratic majorities in the House and Senate should be far more assertive in developing their alternatives to the Nixon administration's legislative program and far more persistent in bringing these alternatives to the public's attention. The simple expedient of a press and communications apparatus for the Democratic congressional parties could make a significant difference in the party's ability to command the national media.

But all of this presupposes some general notions among Democrats as to their common purpose and some shared understandings of their common goals. Not unanimous agreement, by any means, but at least the ability to answer two fundamental questions: Why the Democratic Party? What is the Democratic Party?

Although the Roosevelt coalition has been disintegrating for many years, the party's crisis of identity became acute in the context of the Vietnam War, a conflict escalated by two Democratic administrations and a conflict that the Democratic Party subsequently committed itself to end. The surge of the "new politics" within the party after the 1968 campaign—the wide-ranging reform of its internal rules and procedures, coupled with the Orwellian rewriting of Democratic history—split the party in many ways. But none was more telling than the party's seeming paralysis to sustain the kind of broad-based coalition that is essential to action.

Coalition politics simply will not work in an environment where indictments of past behavior are being handed down or where the party apparatus, such as it is, is being commandeered for one highly controversial objective—the immediate ending of the Vietnam War. What started out as a crusade to broaden the Democratic Party's base by inviting in the anti-war activists who were excluded at Chicago ended as a movement that brought the party its worst presidential defeat in more than two generations.

The most lasting result of the Civil Rights Symposium may, in retrospect, turn out to be the rekindling of the belief that coalition, non-ideological politics worked in the past and that it remains our best hope for renewed progress now. It is wrong to interpret the Nixon landslide as a solid endorsement by the voters of his first-term record, particularly on the domestic side. A permanent Republican majority has not emerged and, in fact, the electorate is very much up for grabs.

Salaried and hourly wage earners—men and women, young and old, black and white—express a sense of uneasiness and dissatisfaction with their lives—the boredom of their jobs, the inequities of the tax system, the continuing welfare mess, the insecurities associated with poor health and old age, the problems of crime and drugs. The political party and political leadership that can speak convincingly to these needs, and, even more importantly, *do* something about them, should very likely emerge as the majority force in American politics for at least the next decade. Given its traditions and instincts, this is an opportunity that the Democratic Party should tackle with relish.

Indeed, one might more accurately describe the symposium as less of a civil rights meeting and more of a political convocation of middle-of-the-road Democrats and their minority group allies, both of whom shared many of the same frustrations and defeats of the last four to six years. Although not totally in agreement on means and ends, both groups left Austin with their self-confidence bolstered and their perspectives sharpened.

The participants could ponder the words of the newly-elected member of the House of Representatives, Barbara Jordan, a black, from a Texas congressional district that is not predominantly black. During Monday afternoon's panel discussion, she was asked whether the civil rights movement had played a significant part in her political success. She answered that it was, at best, a tangential factor in her political career.

"When I first ran for the Texas Senate in 1966, it was with the support of a coalition of good people—white, black, Mexican-American —from a district that was not predominantly black. These people shared my confidence in what was taking place nationally in the civil rights field. This gave us the confidence we needed to run a winning campaign and to keep winning in every election since then," she said.

"The kind of political base that I have built, a black woman in Texas, is the kind of power base that can get this coalition back in shape nationally. It is not dependent upon civil rights, or any single issue. It is based fundamentally on their trust in me, that I'll look out for their interests, whatever their race or color. I have no hesitation whatever in calling for a regeneration of the old coalition that accomplished the gains we have been describing, even though our objectives today are going to be very different and probably more difficult to achieve," she concluded.

• • •

Humphrey and I left for Washington on the 9:00A.M. Braniff flight out of Austin. We missed all of the second day's proceedings, principally Lyndon Johnson's address in which he spoke forcefully about the unequal position of blacks in America due to generations of discrimination and denial and how, in these circumstances, compensatory measures must be taken by white America to close the gap. It is intriguing to speculate whether LBJ, the active President or majority leader, would have chosen the same words as LBJ, the elder stateman.

We also missed the outspoken, but exceedingly polite, "disruption" of the symposium by Roy Innis of CORE and the Rev. A. Kendall Smith of the Beulah Baptist Church of New York City, uninvited black separatists who demanded to be heard. Upon the conclusion of their remarks, and after the NAACP's Clarence Mitchell proclaimed that "If President Johnson has the courage to come out and speak against white demagoguery, I have the duty to come out and speak against black demagoguery." Lyndon Johnson rose again to speak extemporaneously, urging the participants to agree on a program of goals and take them directly to President Nixon.

"There is no point in starting off by saying he is terrible because he doesn't think he is terrible. He doesn't want to leave the Presidency believing that he has been unfair," Johnson said.

While this exchange was taking place in Austin, Humphrey, at 32,000 ft., was talking about his hopes of convening an informal group of senators, Democrats and Republicans, and a number of symposium participants to begin exploring the specific steps that might, over time, build a more formidable coalition in support of a renewed attack on the domestic front.

"I think we have to try," Humphrey said, "even if we don't know exactly what steps should be taken or who should take the lead. It's almost like starting at the beginning when you look back to what we did in the early fifties. But the worse thing of all would be to do nothing."

He kept talking. "So much depends on ending the war, for the country and certainly for the Democratic Party. Democrats, in particular, are literally going to be hamstrung until we are free of the burden of the war.

Once U.S. involvement has ended, we'll have a chance to find ourselves again, to get our bearings, and to begin pulling together the political forces that could make a difference in the next four years.

"You know," he said, "I found tremendous life in the Democratic Party all through the primaries. This business about the Democratic Party being dead is nonsense. Most people I found were sensible people who wanted to get things back together again. They were tired of reading people out of the party. They wanted to begin pulling them back in, at least in the sense of making the party an instrument for appealing to a broad constituency and in terms of bread-and-butter issues."

"The Democrats have to take the lead," he continued, "and we can pick up allies among the Republicans, just as we did in 1964 and 1965 on the civil rights bills. But we've got to get things going and we can, once that damn war is over."

At that point, seemingly to confirm Humphrey's observation about Republican allies, a young man crossed the aisle of the plane and introduced himself as Stanley Pottinger, then assistant secretary for civil rights in the Department of Health, Education and Welfare and, more recently, nominated to be the assistant attorney general for civil rights in the Department of Justice. He, too, had been in Austin for the symposium and was returning to Washington.

Pottinger asked Humphrey if he could stop by his office after Congress had convened in January. "I thought your speech made a lot of sense and I'd like to follow up with you if I could," he said.

Humphrey replied that he would be glad to see him. And after Pottinger returned to his seat, I said something to Humphrey about "any port in a storm."

Humphrey smiled. "You'd get pretty darn lonesome if you were over there, wouldn't you? We've got to make him feel welcome. And a lot of other people, as well."

• • •

AFTERWORD

Many years have passed since most of the events described in these pages took place. The Promised Land is a distant memory, all but lost in the mists of history.

For one thing, there has been a profound erosion of the assumptions that were the bedrock for so many of the events—both successes and failures—that caught my attention forty years ago. One assumption, in particular, that motivated and guided Hubert Humphrey and his wide circle of allies was captured by Clinton Rossiter, the great professor of American government at Cornell, with these words: "No America without democracy; no democracy without politics; no politics without parties; no parties without compromise and moderation." Looking back on the George W. Bush administration and the exceedingly nasty presidential campaign of 2004, one encounters, instead of compromise and moderation, ever-larger doses of acrimony, absolutism, and radical conservatism, often supported by distortion and demagoguery.

Interwoven with these behaviors is an overlay of religious sanctimony and moral certainty used to justify arrogance and rigidity in policy development and execution. Despite the often overwhelming evidence of the need for change of direction in a host of domestic and international areas, opposition views, however constructive in nature, usually have been characterized as unpatriotic or, even worse, un-Christian. Although President Bush and his adherents rarely say it quite this baldly, their claims, for example, to be the most reliable defenders of "family values" in American life easily translates to born-again Christians as assurance that their brand of evangelical Christianity is alive and well in the Oval Office. For many, the unstated corollary to this proposition is that Bush's opponents, in some way or another, have to be regarded as knowing or unknowing surrogates of the Devil.

Author Ron Suskind quotes Bruce Bartlett, domestic policy adviser to Ronald Reagan and the first President Bush, on this point. Bartlett observes: "He truly believes he's on a mission from God. Absolute faith like that overwhelms a need for analysis. The whole thing about faith is to believe things for which there is no empirical evidence . . . But you can't run the world on faith." (*NY Times* Magazine, October 17, 2004, p. 46)

This injection of sanctimonious Christianity and self-satisfied religiosity into American political life would have distressed Reinhold Niebuhr and most *C&C* readers beyond measure. Indeed, they would have branded George Bush's easy association of his presidency and its major decisions with some manner of divine intervention as bordering on blasphemy. The thunder of their denunciations would have resonated loudly from the pages of *C&C*.

Niebuhr's daughter, Elizabeth Sifton, has captured many of these concerns in her recent biographical account of her father, *The Serenity Prayer: Faith & Politics in Times of Peace & War* (W.W. Norton, 2003). She notes Niebuhr's observation about America's growing dependency on nuclear weapons in the aftermath of World War II. Niebuhr observed: "We might remember the prophetic warnings to the nations of old, that nations which become proud because they were divine instruments must, in turn, stand under the divine judgment and be destroyed . . . if ever a nation needed to be reminded of the perils of vainglory, we are that nation. . . ." (307–308) Bush's repeated linking of the Iraq War with a divinely inspired expansion of freedom across the globe surely qualifies a vainglorious twenty-first century America as a fit candidate for Niebuhr's reminder of divine judgment.

Because the dangers of unheeding human pride are inevitably part of any political endeavor, Niebuhr's famous aphorism from *The*

Children of Light and the Children of Darkness rings with special clarity today: "Man's capacity for justice makes democracy possible; but man's inclination to injustice makes democracy necessary." Rossiter's linkage of the survival of American democracy to political compromise and moderation is the logical extension of Niebuhr's famous pronouncement.

Sifton captures the political and moral consequences of Niebuhr's religious thinking. She writes in *The Serenity Prayer:* "Nations, like all communities, like any church or political gathering, cannot presume an absolute claim on truth, rectitude, virtue, force, or power. Democratic debate . . . was an essential component in the formulation of policies and plans, he [Niebuhr] believed, for democracy's leaders must always take account of the contingent human errors that will inevitably alter what we do. Open, tolerant, engaged respect for the differences among us is essential. There is no freedom without it . . . ." (316) The reluctance of President Bush and his associates to admit even one error or mistake and their habit of receiving constructive criticism as evidence only of disloyalty represents, at the end of the day, a willingness to drive a stake through the heart of American democracy.

Another striking change from what I observed forty years ago has to do with the decline of civility in political discourse. At root, civility is simply respect for individuals, regardless of differences over policy. It is listening and dialogue—the kind Humphrey stimulated during the seventy-five day great debate surrounding passage of the Civil Rights Act of 1964. It is understanding that acceptance of a diversity of viewpoints has been a sustaining element of our democratic experiment from the beginning, even during those moments when prejudice and suppression of unpopular opinions seemed to rule the day.

The decline of civility in our public life—captured most audibly in the daily rantings of conservative talk show hosts—coupled with erosion of moderation and compromise in the conduct of the nation's public business has produced a growing polarization of America. There are red states and blue states and people who are most concerned about "moral values" and then everyone else. There are unquestioning patriots and the flip-floppers. George Bush received more votes for president in 2004 than anyone in American history. But he also had more votes cast against him than any other incumbent president. This polarization undoubtedly is a key ingredient in the erosion of trust in American governmental institutions that has come to pass over the last forty years.

It is hard to believe but the Survey Research Center of the University of Michigan in 1964 found that 64 percent of Americans believed that "the government is pretty much run for the benefit of all the people." Even more amazing today is the similar finding in 1964 that 77 percent of Americans believed that the government in Washington can be trusted to do what is right "just about always or most of the time." How can one today explain the extraordinary loss of the people's trust in their government that has taken place? How does one begin to repair this enormous rent in the fabric of democracy?

Four decades ago mainline religious faiths and denominations played a crucial role in mobilizing the grass-roots support that helped pass the Civil Rights Act of 1964 and the Voting Rights Act of 1965. In 2004, conservative evangelical Christians were at the front of the line battling the notion of same-gender marriages, abortion, and gun control. Many of us applauded the linkage of politics and religion in the mid-1960s but were appalled by what unfolded in the 2004 election. Isn't this a clear double standard? How can it be defended?

This much can be said: Religious activism in support of civil rights legislation arose from a determination to expand freedom and personal liberty of persons who had been denied these rights for centuries. Evangelical Christians engaged in political action often seek the opposite: a restriction on personal liberty, not to mention simple justice, for same-gender couples and restricting personal decisions on abortion. The bottom line is less freedom, less liberty, less justice for some of our fellow citizens. Where are the Christian values in this equation?

Many Christians at the forefront of the civil rights struggle also were acutely aware of the inherent limits to wisdom and certainty in all human endeavors, and that ultimately we are all sinners to be saved by grace. They understood the dangers of excessive pride. Humphrey never attacked the motives of the Southern Democrats even as he strongly disagreed with them. Many contemporary evangelicals entertain no such doubts. They are absolutely certain in their beliefs and that persons not sharing these views are, more than likely, damned for eternity. Niebuhr would find this linkage between religion and politics profoundly anti-Democratic, as well as blasphemous in terms of Christian theology. Indeed, these four decades have been deeply troubling to the Christian activists who were the mainstay of *C&C* and the civil rights struggle.

Many other, less momentous, things have changed. Computer technology and the Internet were not even imagined by most of us forty years ago. Secretaries still typed multiple copies of everything and cut stencils for mimeograph machines. Long distance calls were an event. And these calls were placed on dial telephones. We watched black and white TV and sent telegrams. Newspapers were the prime source of news and information for most people. Who could even imagine a non-stop twenty-four-hour news cycle?

The current communications environment, compared to what we knew four decades ago, places a premium on instant access, confrontation, sound bites, personal attack, intimidation, acrimony, and punditry—all seemingly designed to impede rather than foster development of wise and effective policies. Is it any wonder that today a whopping 9 percent of Americans are found by the Gallup Poll to have a great deal of trust and confidence in the mass media, less than half the percentage that was recorded ten years ago?

This Afterword is being written in the immediate aftermath of George Bush's election to a second term. How will he choose to lead and govern? He decided to pursue a radical right-wing agenda following his 2000 triumph when he didn't have a mandate. His behavior during the first term greatly increased the level of polarization in America. Now that he at least enjoys a majority in both the Electoral College and the popular vote—but still no real mandate—one can only look to the second term with concern and unease.

What is to be done? That is a subject for another place and time. Perhaps a sequel to *One Last Chance* is in order. Then, in 1974, I examined two imperatives facing the Democrats, arising out of the Johnson Administration and coming to full flower under Nixon: "*. . . first, to restore the popular belief that government—especially the Federal government—can function competently and fairly; second, to convince people that government cares about what happens to average citizens.*" (159) The central conclusion of that effort, now three decades old, still has the ring of relevance.

Moreover, getting this message through to disaffected middle-class voters remains a central challenge for Democrats. During the Nixon years, Democrats struggled to reach out to the "silent majority." Then, reclaiming the allegiance of "Reagan Democrats" became a major challenge. Today, communicating with the advocates of "family values," both Protestants and Catholics, is near the top of the Democratic recovery agenda. One thing seems clear: The Democrats' advantage on economic, health, and environmental issues is largely blunted if evangelical Christians and conservative Catholics simply refuse to entertain these issues due to their deep alienation on matters of faith and religion. Thomas Frank, in his recent book, *What's the Matter With Kansas: How Conservatives Won the Heart of America* (Metropolitan Books, 2004), has painstakingly explained how so-called family value issues repeatedly overwhelm the economic self-interest of such voters, even when the Republican conservatives they elect focus their efforts, time and again, almost exclusively on expanding the wealth of the wealthy while ignoring these "family value" imperatives except at election time.

Democrats need to figure out ways at least to be heard by voters who lead faith-centered lives and also struggle to make ends meet. Democrats have to join their conversation. Communicating a sense of concern has a lot to do with it. One can recognize and respect their determination to raise their children in traditional ways, worship in non-traditional ways, do home schooling, or attend NASCAR races without agreeing with them on highly incendiary matters, such as same-gender marriages or abortion. *One can listen respectfully to what they have to say.* That appears to have been the approach of Barack Obama, the self-described "skinny kid with the funny name," who won significant support from conservatives in Southern Illinois in his highly successful 2004 campaign for the U.S. Senate. At the same time, Democrats can be making the case that "family values" surely involve the chance to hold a good job, have access to reliable medical care, and the right to breath clean air and drink good water.

Communicating real concern about the struggles of life—listening to what social conservatives have to say—in the end reflects a civility and an avoidance of exclusivity and pride among Democrats that surely would hearten Reinhold Niebuhr. Over time, this approach would likely achieve among some evangelical Christians and conservative Catholics a willingness at least to listen to what Democrats have to say. And that is the essential first step in getting the currently disaffected to consider the range of issues—including such self-interested concerns as a growing economy, accessible health care, and a clean environment—that ultimately can influence behavior on election day. Sooner or later, these bedrock issues—major factors in determining how families live—can win again for the Democrats.

In no way is this to suggest that the challenges facing those who retain a belief in the underpinnings of American democracy as set forth by Rossiter and Niebuhr, and as put into practice by Humphrey and many of his contemporaries, are anything but immense and daunting. But, at the end of the day, there is still hope.

Last June (2004), I was invited by the U.S. Department of Justice's Civil Rights Division to participate on a panel of elders to discuss the Civil Rights Act of 1964 as part of a symposium to honor its passage forty years ago. I accepted the invitation with some trepidation, not knowing exactly what to expect from Attorney General Ashcroft's associates. My assignment was to describe how the legislation passed the Senate in the face of the Southern Democratic filibuster that had never been defeated in prior battles. I recounted many of the details set forth earlier in this volume, especially underscoring the importance of bipartisanship and Humphrey's determination to let everyone, even the bill's opponents, have an opportunity to present their case in an environment free of intimidation. My presentation was well received.

I then decided to add a postscript. I had thought hard about the wisdom of doing so but decided, in the end, that I could not pass up the opportunity. This is what I told the Department of Justice employees assembled in the Great Hall of the main building on Constitution Avenue:

"As we have been discussing this morning, America is at its best when it expands the boundaries of freedom and personal liberty. That is why we honor passage of the Civil Rights Act of 1964 and the people who won its passage. We all know this is true. That is why I must express my deep personal distress at the efforts of persons of responsibility in our government, and in this building, of proposing to use the U.S. Constitution as a vehicle to restrict the personal freedoms and liberty of certain of our fellow Americans. I have tried but cannot find a way to distinguish discrimination and denial of liberty based on skin color and discrimination and denial of liberty based on sexual orientation. That is why I find current proposals to outlaw same-gender marriages by constitutional amendment to be an affront to the great principles of justice captured in the Civil Rights Act and enshrined in the Constitution. I know this statement may be considered rude or out of place by some persons here. But I feel these concerns need to be voiced. So I have spoken."

I did not know what to expect. Frosty indifference? Heated denunciation? Deportation to Guantanamo? Who could tell? But I never expected what, in fact, happened.

The audience of Department of Justice employees rose to its feet, almost as one, with a loud and sustained ovation. The clapping went on for some time. And when the panel adjourned, many employees with essentially this message approached me: "We are so glad you said what you said. It needed to be said but we could never do it. We'd be fired for sure. Thank you for speaking up."

If that can happen in John Ashcroft's Great Hall in the Department of Justice, there is, indeed, hope.